W9-BXD-520

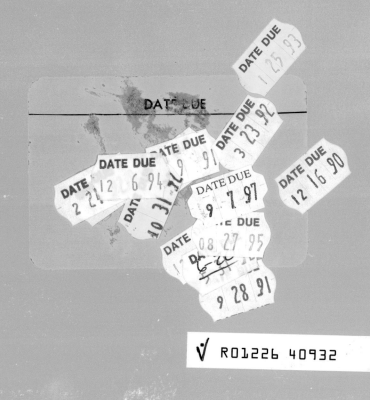

DATE DUE

DATE DUE 1 25 93

DATE DUE 3 23 92

DATE DUE 3

DATE DUE 9 91

DATE DUE

DATE 2 21

12 6 94

10 31

DATE DUE 9 7 97

DATE DUE 12 16 90

DATE DUE 08 27 95

DATE

DA

9 28 91

SHAKESPEARE'S STORIES
Comedies

Retold by Beverley Birch

Illustrated by Carol Tarrant
Cover illustration: Nick Harris

PETER BEDRICK BOOKS
NEW YORK

First American edition published in 1988 by
Peter Bedrick Books, New York

Published by agreement with Macdonald & Co. (Publishers) Ltd., London.
A member of Pergamon MCC Publishing Corporation plc.

Library of Congress Cataloging-in-Publication Data
Birch, Beverley.
    Shakespeare's stories: comedies/retold by Beverley Birch;
illustrated by Carol Tarrant; cover illustration, Nick Harris. –
1st American ed.
        p.   cm.
    Contents: The taming of the shrew – Much ado about nothing –
Twelfth night – A midsummer night's dream – The tempest.
    ISBN 0–87226–191–3
    1. Shakespeare, William, 1564–1616 – Adaptations – Juvenile
literature. 2. Shakespeare, William, 1564–1616 – Comedies – Juvenile
literature. [1. Shakespeare, William, 1564–1616 – Adaptations.]
I. Shakespeare, William, 1564–1616.   II. Tarrant, Carol, ill. III. Title.
PR2877.B44 1988
813'.54–dc19   88–16947
                                                                                CIP
                                                                                AC

Printed in Great Britain
10 9 8 7 6 5 4 3 2 1

Series Editor: Luigi Bonomi
Series Design: Sylvia Kwan
Production: Rosemary Bishop

The author's grateful thanks are due to Priscilla Stone for her perceptive
comment, criticism and never-flagging encouragement, and to Ruairidh
and Calum MacLean, who have tirelessly read the scripts with the
healthy scepticism of a young eye, and whose comments have been a
source of inspiration and much-valued guidance.

-CONTENTS-

A Midsummer Night's Dream

How slow the old moon waned! Four days until the bright new moon brought in the wedding day of great Duke Theseus. Four days to watch the old moon lingering and dream of pleasures yet to come. But with what triumph, pomp and celebration then would Theseus marry fair Hippolyta beneath the new moon's silver bow: though he had wooed and won her with the sword, now he would wed this Queen of Amazons with mirth and merriment and revelling through all of Athens.

There were others who watched the passage of the waning moon with anxious eyes. There was a girl of Athens named Hermia, whose father wanted her to wed Demetrius, a rich and handsome youth most suitable as a husband. But Hermia did not love Demetrius. She loved Lysander, also rich and handsome, but to young Hermia's eyes, so much finer than any other youth. Lysander had won her heart with poetry, by moonlight sung of love, showered her with tokens of his adoration, flowers, rings and locks of hair . . .

The father stormed against his daughter, who with her passionate tongue and stubborn disobedience, refused Demetrius and declared her love for young Lysander. He came in anger to Duke Theseus to demand the law against his rebellious child. Either she should marry the man *he* chose, or suffer the punishment decreed by law: death, or live out her days far from the company of men, locked in a nunnery.

Duke Theseus gave Hermia until the next new moon, his wedding day, to make her choice. On that day she must declare herself: either to marry Demetrius, as her father wished, or let the laws of Athens take their course.

The lovers would not yield. To be forced to choose their love through other's eyes! Rather, they would flee the laws of Athens, and marry without a father or a duke's consent!

So they agreed, and in a wood outside the walls of Athens they arranged to meet, the following night, by moonlight . . .

Demetrius, though fiercely scorned by Hermia, yet loved her passionately. But he was adored by another girl of Athens: Helena. Helena was Hermia's closest friend: since childhood they had played and shared together.

But now Helena, who loved Demetrius with all her body and soul, found that he merely spurned her passionate devotion, and emptied all his love on her *friend* Hermia! He had eyes only for Hermia's dark eyes, ears only for Hermia's rich voice. The more *Hermia* frowned on him, the more he loved her! The more *Hermia* showed her hate, the more he followed her.

While she, poor loving Helena, found only that the more *she* followed Demetrius, the more he hated her!

There was no sense or fairness in love's choices! Hermia was small and strong and dark with deep brown eyes and raven hair. Helena was tall and slim and fair with soft blue eyes. Many in Athens (as Helena told herself) considered her no less beautiful than Hermia, and before Demetrius had loved Hermia, he had poured out vows of love to *Helena*. When he saw Hermia these vows vanished like the dew before the rising sun, and left poor Helena trailing like a discarded pet.

But Helena would not give up, and she was desperate to find some favour, however small, in Demetrius' eyes. Learning from Hermia and Lysander of their plan to flee from Athens the following night, she resolved to tell Demetrius and lead him to where the lovers had arranged to meet, by moonlight in the wood.

These final days of the slow-waning moon had others in a flurry besides our tangled lovers.

In a workman's house in Athens six men were gathered, six honest, earnest, hard-working men of that great city. There was Peter Quince the carpenter, Francis Flute the bellow's mender, Tom Snout the tinker, Robin Starveling the tailor, Snug the joiner; and last, but by no means least, Nick Bottom the weaver.

They planned a most important event for the celebrations of Duke Theseus's wedding day: a play, performed by them. And what a play their play would be! A story of tragic lovers such as there had never

7

been in all the world: 'The most lamentable comedy and cruel death of Pyramus and Thisby': a very good piece of work, Bottom assured the assembled company, and helpfully urged Peter Quince to start by calling them, man by man, according to the parts that they would play.

Bottom the weaver was, in the eyes of all who knew him, a most worthy man, a man of many parts and many talents, a man who, amongst all the quantities of working men in Athens, *must* play Pyramus, the lover that kills himself for love . . .

Bottom was pleased with this. Why, it would call for a truly *dramatic* performance. It would draw tears in torrents from the audience, though he confessed he was more disposed to play a tyrant, for a tyrant could rant and rave. He leapt to his feet and bellowed lustily,

'The raging rocks
And shivering shocks
Shall break the locks
Of prison gates . . .'

Now this was a part a man was made for! (A lover, he assured his friends, was more condoling . . .)

Francis Flute was none too pleased to have to play the lady's part, for he had a beard coming.

'Let me play Thisby too!' cried Bottom with considerable relish. 'I'll speak in a monstrous little voice. "Thisne, Thisne,"' he demonstrated his tiny squeak with much flapping of 'elegant' lady's wrists, '"Pyramus my lover dear! Thy Thisby dear and lady dear!"'

The other parts were distributed with greater speed, for Bottom's imagination was not truly captured by mere fathers or mothers of the tragic lovers. But the *lion* – that was a part! If Snug the joiner was nervous of it, Bottom would do it! He would roar such a roar that the Duke would say 'Let him roar again!' Or, if that frightened the ladies in the audience, he could roar as gently as a dove, as sweetly as a nightingale . . .

It was, however, firmly established by good Peter Quince (who manfully wrestled control of the proceedings from the enthusiastic weaver), that Bottom must play *Pyramus*. This Pyramus was as sweet-faced a man as any you would see on a summer's day, a most gentleman-like man . . .

Bottom's thoughts had turned to the question of the beard. What beard should Pyramus wear, he mused. Your straw-coloured beard?

Your orange-tawny beard? Your purple-in-grain beard, your French crown-coloured beard, your perfect yellow?

With some effort, Quince managed to move on, for he had a final, most important communication to impart to his attentive company. They must *learn their lines*. By tomorrow night, they must all know them well. (Snug took this particularly seriously, for he was slow to learn, and was concerned to get the lion's roaring right.)

And so as not to have the whole of Athens know their plans, they would rehearse their play in secret. In the woods outside the town, they would all meet the following night, by moonlight . . .

The wood lay silver-tipped beneath the moon, each blade of grass, each leaf and branch soft-stroked with liquid pearl. It was a place of whisperings and shimmerings, of watching eyes green-glowing like fire beneath the giant trees.

It was a place of magic. It was bewitched by more than the moon's caress across the darkened glades.

It was the realm of Oberon, King of Fairies, and of Titania, his silver queen. No human eye could see them, no human ear could hear them, but they were there, woven in the rugged oaks that bowed across the moon-washed world, threaded in the murmuring earth, floating on the lilt of brooks and the sweet wind that sighed across the leaves.

And tonight this wood was haunted by more than the joyous revels of fairies, elves and sprites, for it trembled beneath the King of Fairies' anger at the Fairy Queen.

Titania had, as her attendant, a lovely human boy taken from an Indian king. How she loved and cherished this changeling child! But Oberon was jealous: he desired the boy to be a knight of his train, to wander the wild forests with *him* . . .

And now these proud and passionate monarchs never met on hill or dale, in forest grove or meadow green, but that their bitter quarrel soured the air, poisoned the winds and turned the earth to misery. Because of them dark fogs and bitter frosts had wrapped the warmth of spring in winter's shroud; unripe corn lay rotting in the field, and swollen rivers drowned the meadows and the villages.

And still Oberon demanded the changeling boy to be his henchman, and still Titania withheld him, crowned him with flowers and made him all her joy. Now, though they flew from the far corners of the earth to

9

bring their blessings to Duke Theseus' wedding day, still their old
quarrel flared anew . . .

'Ill met by moonlight, proud Titania!' Oberon hailed her, and the
great oaks trembled with the anger of this powerful lord of the dark
place, while all his tiny elves drew close behind their master.

Titania's fairies peeped from the silver glow that wrapped their
dancing queen.

'What, jealous Oberon,' Titania cried. 'Fairies, skip away. I have
foresworn his bed and company!'

He stepped towards her, fierce. 'Why should Titania cross her

Oberon?' he challenged her again. 'I do but beg a little changeling boy to be my henchman!'

'The fairy land buys not the child from me!' Titania sang and danced away from the dark thunder of her husband's eyes. 'His mother was of my following; for her sake I do rear up her boy, and for her sake I will not part with him!' And away she flew, her lilting voice echoing in Oberon's ears with mocking taunt.

He brooded on her disobedience, and the brooding filled his soul. *She* would not leave this forest glade till he had tormented her for his injury! He called his attendant to him, a shrewd, prick-eared goblin known as Puck, much given to pranks and roguish tricks. To him, the King of Fairies gave his secret orders. There was a tiny purple flower called 'love-in-idleness' that grew far off in the western lands . . .

'Fetch me that flower,' he breathed. 'The juice of it laid on sleeping eyelids will make man or woman madly love the next live creature that it sees. I'll watch Titania when she is asleep, and drop the liquid on her eyes. The next thing that she, waking, looks upon, be it lion, bear, wolf or bull, meddling monkey or busy ape, she shall pursue it with the soul of love . . . Fetch me this herb, and be here again before the whale can swim a league!'

'I'll put a girdle round about the earth in forty minutes!' chanted Puck, and disappeared.

And Oberon brooded on his plan; while Titania languished in bewitchment, he could spirit away the changeling boy . . .

But Oberon's mischievous thoughts were suddenly and violently disturbed: a raucous clamour tore the air, the sound of quarreling *human* voices, the crash of *human* feet! Being invisible, he hovered close to hear these rash intruders entering his domain.

It was Demetrius, blundering through the undergrowth in search of Hermia. But he was followed, as he always was, by love-lorn Helena. In vain he tried to shake her off. He yelled. He frowned. He shouted. But she was there, her love-sick gaze still drinking in each word and look of his as though they were the nectar of the gods themselves.

'I cannot love you!' he shouted, for perhaps the hundredth time.

'And even for that I do love you more,' she sobbed. 'I am your slave, the more you beat me, I will fawn on you. Use me but as your slave, spurn me, strike me, neglect me, only give me leave to follow you . . .'

'I am sick when I must look at you,' the desperate youth declared.

'And I am sick when I look not at you,' the wretched girl replied.

And Oberon, festering with his own lovers' quarrel, was touched by the unhappy Helena's plight. He vowed a second vow that night: before Helena could leave his forest realm, Demetrius would seek *her* love and she would fly from *him*.

Now Puck alighted at his side and held aloft the magic flower. Oberon seized it. It caught a glancing moonbeam and gleamed purple in the cloaking dark. He stroked it, murmuring, and the wind took up his words and sowed them in the trees . . . 'I know a bank where the wild thyme blows, where oxlips and the nodding violet grows. There sleeps Titania sometime of the night, lulled in these flowers . . .'

And then, with sudden anger he cried out, 'With the juice of this I'll streak her eyes and make her full of hateful fantasies!'

His gaze now fell on eager Puck, ever ready to follow his master's wish. 'Take some of it,' he ordered him. 'Seek through this grove. A sweet Athenian lady is in love with a disdainful youth. Anoint his eyes with this, and do it when the next thing that he spies will be the lady. You shall know the man by the Athenian clothes that he has on.'

Titania slept, while fairy sentinels drooped drowsily and did not see the Fairy King creep close to her, nor see him squeeze the magic juice across her eyes, nor hear his murmured words . . .

'What thou seest when thou dost wake,
Do it for thy true love take
Love and languish for his sake
Be it lynx, or cat, or bear
Leopard, or boar with bristled hair.
Wake when some vile thing is near.'

Below the sleeping Fairy Queen two other lovers came into the glade: Lysander and the beautiful Hermia, now much begrimed and stuck with twigs and leaves. They had lost their way in this strange wood, and now they were foot-sore and desperately craved sleep. In the morning, fresh, they could resume their flight from Athens.

'Good night, sweet friend,' Hermia whispered to Lysander. 'May your love never alter until your sweet life ends.'

'Amen to that fair prayer,' the loving youth replied. 'And let my life end when I end loyalty . . .'

They settled down together in that dappled glade (but not too close together, till the bonds of marriage were tied up). And so it came about that wandering Puck, seeking Demetrius and Helena, now came upon *this* sleeping couple. He noted the youth's Athenian clothes and the young woman lying some little way away: at once he assumed *this* was the young woman so churlishly rejected by the youth that Oberon had seen. Swiftly he poured the magic juice across Lysander's eyes, and sped back to his master's side.

For a moment the glade was quiet. And then the crashing in the undergrowth began again; into the glade stumbled frantic Demetrius, still running from a more than frantic Helena. With a final furious shout at her, he plunged on into the wood, so that she stood now, quite alone amid the looming trees.

It seemed now that no plea, no prayer could work its charm on scornful Demetrius, and Helena despaired. She ached with tiredness. She slipped and slithered in the dark, seeking a place where she could sink to rest. As she did, she stumbled across sleeping Lysander. Afraid he might be hurt, she shook the youth, and Lysander, waking with his eyes streaked with the magic juice, saw Helena and fell instantly, passionately in love. All thoughts of Hermia took flight (how tedious seemed the hours spent with her). Who could still love a raven such as Hermia beside this glowing, dove-like Helena?

Helena stared at Lysander now in greater misery than ever before. What had she done to draw this mockery from others? It was not enough for Demetrius to spurn her, but Lysander must add to her injuries by playing his own games with her! It was too much for any girl to bear! And Helena rushed frantically from the glade, Lysander in hot pursuit of this, his most passionate new love.

Hermia, quite ignorant of the magic changes in her lover's heart, slept on, until a dream of crawling serpents woke her violently. Alone? Lysander gone? No answering shout to greet her? Only a thousand night creatures' glinting eyes!

In terror she ran off, shrieking for Lysander . . .

To this same wood, at midnight, came the six working men of Athens, prepared to do their play exactly as they would before Duke Theseus. They tramped into the moonlit glade and looked around (a little apprehensively, if each were to admit it to the other).

'Here's a marvellous convenient place for our rehearsal,' Quince declared. 'This green plot shall be our stage, this hawthorn bush our dressing room.'

Bottom had been thinking very seriously. 'There are things in this comedy of Pyramus and Thisby that will never please,' he told them, soberly. 'First, Pyramus must draw a sword to kill himself, which the ladies of the audience cannot abide . . .'

Snout, Starveling and Flute all nodded: the killing must, undoubtedly, be quite left out.

Bottom had pondered his way towards a better answer. They must have an introduction to their play – a *prologue* – (he said the word proudly to give it full effect) – and this prologue would say that they would do no harm with their swords, and that Pyramus was not really killed, and (to reassure them thoroughly) Pyramus was not *really* Pyramus, but Bottom the weaver.

An excellent solution!

In the trees about their makeshift stage there lurked an unseen watcher who observed their earnest efforts with amusement.

'What hempen homespuns have we swaggering here, so near the cradle of the fairy queen?' bright Puck enquired, for his mischievous nose had sniffed out the flavour of some teasing frolic for his entertainment.

Unknowing of their hidden audience, the players now began. Bottom, as Pyramus, was first. 'Thisby, the flowers of odious savours sweet,' he declared, most eloquently.

'Odours, odours,' interrupted Quince.

'Odours savours sweet,' said Bottom obligingly. 'But hark! A voice!' and right on cue, he disappeared into the hawthorn bush.

There was a silence. All eyes turned expectantly to Francis Flute. It dawned on him, though slowly, that they were all waiting for *him*.

'Must I speak now?' he asked, nervously.

'Aye,' said Quince, most patiently. 'Pyramus goes but to see a noise, and will come again.'

Promptly (before he lost his nerve), Flute spewed out all his lines at once in a great flood, and left nothing more to speak in the rest of the play.

Quince sighed deeply: 'You must not speak that yet,' he said, in a tone of utmost world-weariness, 'Pyramus, enter!' he called. 'Your cue is past . . .'

But hovering Puck had suddenly devised the merriest prank of all. Following Bottom into the hawthorn bush, he had swiftly touched the weaver's ears, which, in no more than the blinking of a goblin's eye became long, furry, flapping ears; his nose, which grew into a long, bony nose; his eyes, which became the large, dark, somewhat bewildered eyes of an enormous, hairy ass!

Bottom, unaware of this miraculous transformation, reappeared at Quince's call with gusto.

'If I were fair, Thisby,' he announced with passion, 'I were only yours!'

His companions stared. They blinked. They backed away. They trembled. And then, with one panic-stricken howl, they fled.

Somewhat bewildered, Bottom watched his friends run out, run back again, stare, shriek, point fingers, gibber, peer at him from behind the trees and disappear again . . .

Why did they run? Some joke of theirs, to come and gawp and run again!

'Bless you, bless you, Bottom, bless you!' Quince whispered in awe. 'You are translated!'

This was unmistakeably a ruse to frighten him, Bottom decided. If only they could! He looked about him at the giant trees, standing sentinel about the grove. They loomed, they leaned . . .

He shook himself. 'I will not stir from this place,' he declared. 'Do what they can, I will not stir. I will walk up and down here. And I will sing. And they shall hear I am not afraid!' this last he yelled defiantly across the silent grove. And he burst forth,

'The ousel cock so black of hue
With orange-tawny bill
The throstle . . .'

Cushioned on her bed of flowers, Titania stirred, then stretched and woke. And as she did, her eyes, charmed by the flower-juice, fell on this valiant figure with the head of a great ass and body of a sturdy, somewhat portly, man; and instantly this queen of gossamer light fell wildly, insanely, in love with him.

'What angel wakes me from my flowery bed?' she breathed.

The object of her adoration stamped on across the grove, thump, thump, thump, thump; then back again, clump, clump, clump, clump, and then he bellowed even louder to warn the looming shades of night

15

they could not threaten him.

'The finch, the sparrow and the lark
The plain-song cuckoo grey . . .' he carolled.

And then he stopped, for now he saw the silver vision decked in moonbeams float across the grove, and heard her, with a voice like tinsel bells of flowers, speak to him . . .

'I pray you, gentle mortal, sing again. Mine ear is much enchanted by thy note. So is mine eye enthralled by thy shape . . . and I am moved to say that I do love thee.'

Bottom was not a man ever at a loss, for long. He prided himself on this. Silver visions who sang of love in moonlit woods notwithstanding, he *would* maintain his true sense of proportion at all times . . .

'I love you,' the lady sang.

'I think, mistress,' he said, sensibly, 'you should have little reason for that; and yet, to say the truth, reason and love keep little company together nowadays . . .'

'Thou art as wise as thou art beautiful,' the wondrous lady murmured.

'Not so, neither,' he assured her, 'but if I had wit enough to get out of this wood . . .'

'Thou shalt not go,' her music voice sang on. 'Thou shalt remain here, for I do *love* thee . . . Therefore go with me,' the lady whispered in his ear (the great, tall ass's ear that twitched a little for her lips were tickling him). And away she drew him, and wove her spells about him: she would give him fairies to attend on him and grant his every wish; he could sleep on heady flowers while their perfumes wafted him to sleep; he could feed on apricots and dewberries, on purple grapes and mulberries, on honeybags stolen from the bumble bees; her fairies would fan moonbeams from his sleeping eyes with wings of butterflies.

Bottom, refusing to be bewildered by the orderly procession of tiny fairies before his eyes, was always a polite man. Each one, in turn, he addressed with courteous concentration, made sure he asked each name, and shook each hand (though this was somewhat difficult with hands that seemed to slip like moonlight through his fingers).

'Tie up my love's tongue,' the silver lady whispered. 'Bring him silently . . .'

Oberon's eyes danced with delight at Titania's new love, for quickly

Puck had flown to tell his master, and to amuse him, too, with tales of how he led the other workmen a merry caper from the woods, scrambling and slithering as they were through briars and thorns to escape that haunted place.

And here, to add to Oberon's delight, came the Athenians. Swiftly the dark king and his impish henchman vanished, to watch the spectacle unseen.

Young Hermia came flying in, pursued by passionate Demetrius. She, though much irritated by the persistence of this unwanted youth, was more concerned at the disappearance of her love, Lysander. A thought struck her: Demetrius had killed him! She rounded on this hapless youth, her dark eyes flashing instant vengeance if this was so.

Demetrius gave up. He was growing a little weary of this chase, for it gave so few rewards. He was exhausted by these endless hours chasing through this endless wood. Foot-weary, and in great ill-humour, he left Hermia to run on, and lay down on the ground, to sleep.

Oberon rounded on the meddling Puck. Demetrius still loved Hermia! He had not shifted his affections to fair Helena!

No, Puck admitted (much amused by this spectacle of squabbling humans), this was not the Athenian he had charmed . . .

'About the wood go swifter than the wind,' Oberon gave orders, angrily. 'Find Helena of Athens. Lead her here, by magic.' And while Puck flew off to do his bidding, Oberon alighted on the ground near Demetrius, and swift as wind he charmed Demetrius' eyes in time for Helena's appearance.

Puck was much enjoying himself, for mischief was the food of life to him. In a twinkling of an eye he was back, to sing,

'Captain of our fairy band,
Helena is here at hand.
And the youth, mistook by me . . .
Lord, what fools these mortals be!'

Two youths, who both loved Hermia, to be translated into two who both loved Helena! No greater fun could Puck imagine!

Helena's bewilderment at Lysander's loud vows of undying love had turned to fierce indignation. She was desperate to get away from him, to escape this cruel mockery. Stumbling in the moonlight across the forest glade, she fell across Demetrius. He woke, and saw the woman he had scorned so bitterly now coloured by the love-flower's enchanted mists.

'Helen, goddess, nymph, perfect, divine!' he cried. 'To what, my love, shall I compare your eyes? Crystal is muddy! Oh, let me kiss this princess of pure white, this seal of bliss!'

Helena fell back in disbelief. They were hell bent to use her for their merriment! It was not enough that Demetrius should hate her, as he had made plain, now he joined with the others to taunt her pitilessly!

'You would not use a gentle lady so,' she begged, 'to vow and swear your love when I am sure you hate me in your hearts. You are both rivals and love Hermia. Now both rivals you mock Helena!'

To simplify this tangled knot, Lysander grandly donated the absent Hermia (whom he no longer loved) to Demetrius.

Demetrius, who had loved Hermia wildly until a few moments ago, now scorned the gift. He loved *Helena*, adored *Helena*, would worship *Helena* for ever more.

Into this hornets' nest came Hermia, still fretting at Lysander's disappearance from her side, yet with his vows of loyalty to her still echoing in her ears. She saw him now and rushed to his side. 'Why did you leave me so unkindly?'

But why should he stay, she heard Lysander's cold and unfamiliar voice. Love drew him on!

She stopped. She looked from him to Helena, from Helena to Demetrius. She heard again these words her ears could not believe. Her own true love's lips now shouting at her to go and leave him, yelling of the *hate* he felt for her!

Helena, watching this extraordinary scene, saw it all clearly now. It was a plot between all three of them! *Hermia* was at the root of it. This *friend*, with whom she had shared all vows of childhood, was locked in conspiracy with these cruel men, to scorn and bait her!

'Oh, is it all forgotten? All school-days' friendship, childhood innocence?' she sobbed.

Hermia stopped the stream of words. 'I do not scorn you, it seems you scorn me!' In disbelief she heard Lysander's voice. 'My love, my life, my soul, fair Helena! Helen I love you, by my life I do.'

And then Demetrius, bristling against his rival, 'I say I love you more than he can do!'

'If you say so,' Lysander shouted, 'withdraw and prove it!'

'Quick, come!' Demetrius yelled, and drew his sword.

18

Now Hermia understood. She rounded on her friend. 'You juggler! You canker-blossom! You thief of love! What, have you come by night and stolen my love's heart from him?'

'You counterfeit! You puppet!' shrieked Helena back, convinced that this was all still part of their dreadful plot.

'Puppet!' bellowed Hermia. 'Now I see she compares our heights! With her personage, her *tall* personage, her height, no less, she has won him!' She danced in rage before her willowy friend. 'And are you grown so high in his esteem because *I* am so dwarfish and so short? How short am I, you painted maypole? Speak! How short am I? I am not so short that my nails can't reach your eyes!'

'Let her not hurt me,' shrieked Helena. 'Let her not strike me. When she is angry she is keen and shrewd. She was a vixen when she went to school, and though she is little, she is fierce!'

'Little again! Nothing but little!' screamed Hermia, and flew at Helena. Lysander thrust shrinking Helena protectively behind him. Demetrius shouted belligerently. 'Do not take Helena's part!' and once again they were circling each other, like spitting cats . . .

And then (so as not to use swords before the ladies) they went off to find a place to fight for Helena's love, still glaring wildly at each other.

Oberon looked at Puck, and his look was like the thunder before it erupted from a glowering sky.

'This is thy negligence!'

'Believe me, King of Shadows,' Puck sang out, 'I mistook . . . Did you not tell me I should know the man by the Athenian garments he had on? I have anointed an Athenian's eyes!' (But, mistake or not, what sport to see these mortals jangling!)

'These mortals seek a place to fight,' bellowed Oberon. 'Hurry and overcast the night with fog, black, black fog to lead these rivals far astray that they may never meet each other! Then crush this herb into Lysander's eye,' and his look allowed no meddling pranks or disobedience this time.

This miserable confusion must be set to rights and Lysander's vision turned from Helena to Hermia again. But haste, haste, for the night was paling fast, and all must be accomplished before the break of dawn . . .

The impish Puck did as his master ordered, gleefully. He danced and floated in the mists, calling now in Demetrius's voice to wandering Lysander, now in Lysander's voice to stumbling Demetrius; now in a bush, a tree, across the brook, now far behind, now far in front, now up, now down, egging each on until their legs grew weary, their flesh stung with pricks and scratches and each separately, ignorant of how close the other stumbled in the mists, lay down to sleep until daybreak could release them from this misery.

And then the ladies came: first, Helena, smeared with mud, her dress in shreds and longing now for nothing but the sunlight's warmth so that she could escape this hideous place and friends who detested her enough to play these cruel jokes. She lay down to sleep.

'Yet but three?' grinned hovering Puck.

'Come one more;
Two of both kinds
Makes up four.
Here she comes, cursed and sad!'

Hermia could go no further. Though she still longed to find Lysander and stop the fight, she was so soaked with dew, so torn with briars that she was almost crawling . . .

20

And she too lay down to sleep.

Now they were ready for Puck's magic: each close together, though they did not know it, each near their chosen love.

He dropped the herb onto Lysander's sleeping eyes.

'On the ground
Sleep sound
I'll apply
To your eye,
Gentle lover, remedy.'

'When you wake
Take true delight
In the sight
Of your former lady's eye.'

Invisible to the lovers' eyes, a stranger company than they could ever imagine now came among them.

'Come sit upon this flowery bed while I caress your cheeks and stick musk-roses in your sleek, smooth head, and kiss your fair, large ears, my gentle joy,' Titania's cooing voice enticed the weaver on.

Bottom was much enjoying this unlooked for holiday from the workaday existence of a sober Athens weaver.

'Where's Peaseblossom?' he asked. 'Scratch my head, good Peaseblossom. Where's Mounsieur Cobweb? Good Mounsieur, fetch me a red-hipped bumble bee on the top of a thistle; and good Mounsieur, bring me the honey bag; and have a care that the honeybag does not break. I would be loathe to have you overflown with a honeybag, signior.' He settled luxuriously into the bower of flowers. 'Where's Monsieur Mustardseed?'

'What's your will?' a tiny voice came to his languid ears.

'Nothing, good Mounsieur,' said Bottom generously, 'but to help Mounsieur Peaseblossom scratch. I must go to the barber's, Mounsieur,' he assured him, seriously, 'for I think I am marvellously hairy about the face . . .'

He yawned. And if the wondrous fairy lady would cease her stroking and allow him, he was now ready to sleep . . .

'Sleep,' her voice was in the wind, and in the leaves, 'and I will wind thee in my arms. So does the woodbine entwine the sweet

honeysuckle . . . Oh, how I love thee! How I do dote on thee!'

And Titania, too, slept, wound round her love. She did not know this passion was the work of jealous Oberon, nor that he had already seized the changeling boy while she lay wrapped in adoration of Bottom the weaver's ass-headed charms.

Their purpose won, two moon-dappled shadows came among the lovers to undo the charms. Oberon bent low across his queen, and spoke the charmed words that would undo the spell that bound her. He called her, gently, 'now, my Titania, wake, my sweet queen.'

She woke, and saw him bending over her, and looked about her, startled. 'My Oberon! What visions I have seen! I thought I loved an ass.'

'There lies thy love,' murmured Oberon, and as she backed in horror from poor Bottom, blissfully ass-headed on the ground, the king of fairies took her hand.

'Come my queen, take hands with me, and rock the ground whereon these sleepers be!' And so these monarchs of the moonlit night joined hands, new-tied in bonds of love, and dancing in a magic circle blessed the sleepy lovers on the ground.

Tomorrow night their fairy dance would bless the triumph of Duke Theseus' wedding day, but as the morning lark raised his shrill cry, they vanished, to follow the shades of night to other lands . . .

With the morning lark came others to that forest glade. Duke Theseus and his bride-to-be Hippolyta were revelling in their long-awaited wedding day. Before daybreak they had risen to follow the hounds and hunting horns into the woods, and they stood now, listening to their swelling music across the hills and valleys. They paused in the sunlit glade to catch the scent of morning in the flowers, and stumbled, much to their surprise, on the four lovers, fast asleep and lying close together on the ground.

'Go bid the huntsman wake them with their horns,' Duke Theseus commanded.

To the triumphant bay of unleashed hounds and bray of horns across the western valley, the startled lovers woke. They stared at the wondering audience, looked at each other, tried to stammer out an explanation of their presence here, but found they could not really find one . . .

'I came with Hermia,' Lysander remembered, suddenly, and turned with love towards her. All memories of adoration felt for Helena had flown with waking sight of Hermia . . .

And by some power which he could not understand, Demetrius now found himself in love with Helena and not with Hermia!

And so they stood there, once four lovers running in a ring about a moonlit wood, now two loving pairs: Lysander and Hermia, Demetrius and Helena who still could not believe her ears were not playing tricks on her when she heard Demetrius' declaration of his love for her before the *Duke*! 'All the faith, the virtue of my heart, the object and the pleasure of my eye is only Helena,' he said!

Duke Theseus saw at once how perfectly the tangled knot had been untied, and how the thorny problems set by Hermia's father were now resolved. It was a splendid outcome for his own, most glorious, wedding day, and he was in no mood to let a father's anger at the thwarting of his wishes mar its pleasures or the happiness of these young people, so in love.

Swiftly he decided. He would overrule the father if he was still disposed to press an unwanted marriage on his reluctant daughter. 'In the temple, by and by with us, these couples shall eternally be knit in marriage,' he said. 'Away with us to Athens! Three and three we'll hold a feast in great solemnity!'

And with his bride-to-be upon his arm, he swept from the sunlit glade, leaving the bewildered lovers quite alone. They looked at each other curiously. Each wondered if the others had heard and seen what they *thought* they had seen in this strange, misty night just passed . . .

'These things seem small and indistinguishable, like far-off mountains turned into clouds,' murmured Demetrius, wonderingly.

'I seem to see these things with parted eye, when everything seems double,' said Hermia.

'And I have found Demetrius, like a jewel, my own,' sang Helena, who could think of nothing else.

'Are you sure that we are awake?' Demetrius still wondered. 'It seems to me that yet we sleep, we dream.'

And yet Duke Theseus *had* been there, *had* bid them follow him to Athens. On that they all agreed.

They linked arms, chattering suddenly like magpies about the night's events, and followed the Duke's party from that forest glade.

The glade was silent now, warm lit by morning sun. Gone were the flitting shadows of the night who flew on moonbeams from tree to tree. Gone were the lovers, babbling of their dream.

The sun blazed down and wrapped the sleeping Bottom in its golden blanket. He dreamed on, and on. He mumbled in his sleep. He murmured softly, laughed, stretched, and laughed again.

And then slowly, he began to wake, luxuriously. 'When my cue comes, call me, and I will answer,' he murmured. 'My next is, "Most fair Pyramus . . ."' He stretched again. Then he sat up. He looked about him. No one there? He called, 'Peter Quince! Flute! Snout! God's my life, stolen away and left me asleep!'

Then he remembered: a woman of silver light who stroked him, loved him, sang to him, and he wafting on sweet beds of flowers, her king! A life of song and drowsy luxury, of idleness beyond his dreams . . . He almost swooned again with memories.

'I have had a most rare vision,' he assured himself. 'I have had a dream, past the wit of man to say what dream it was. I thought I was . . .' he shook the thought away. 'There is no man can tell what,' he announced conclusively to the slumbering wood. 'I thought I had . . .' he began again.

And again he shook his head. 'The eye of man has not heard, the ear of man has not seen, man's hand is not able to taste, his tongue to imagine or his heart to report, what my dream was,' he addressed the brooding oaks . . . and for a moment he was wandering in his dream again, lost in its ecstasies . . .

'I will get Peter Quince to write a ballad of this dream,' he announced with more certainty, 'and it shall be called Bottom's dream, because it has no bottom . . .'

At Quince's house Bottom's friends despaired. A play without Nick Bottom? A play without their Pyramus? Bottom was the Pyramus to beat all Pyramuses, the tragic lover to beat all lovers. They trembled to think what might have happened to him. Had he been carried off by spirits, transformed (before their eyes) into a monster? Or was it all a nightmare they would wake from, happily?

'Where are these lads?' the booming tones of Bottom sang along the street. 'Where are these good fellows?'

They gaped, searched wildly for the ass's head they had last seen on him. Seeing nothing but their good friend's jovial face, they promptly leapt with joy, clapped him on the back, danced several jigs around him, and all at once there was a flurry of excited preparations.

Costumes ready? Strings to their beards? 'Let Thisby have clean clothes,' urged Bottom enthusiastically. 'And let him that plays the lion not cut his nails, for they shall hang out like the lion's claws. And, most dear actors,' he called them back, 'eat no onions nor garlic, for we are to utter sweet breath; and I do not doubt but to hear them say, it is a sweet

25

comedy. No more words! Away! Go! Away!'

The lovers came now, wed, to while away the hours before their wedding night with jovial entertainment: and a jovial entertainment it certainly promised to be : 'A tedious brief scene of young Pyramus and his love Thisby; very tragical mirth,' the company of actors announced themselves.

The young couples settled comfortably, prepared to be much amused by the efforts of these earnest working men who had so worked to bring this 'tragic' tale to Theseus's celebration.

They little knew what scenes of mirthful tragedy *they* had played before another audience in a silver wood not so very far away . . .

Wall came first. With trembling wide-eyed face above the chink made by his parted fingers, he explained this was the hole through which the tragic lovers, Pyramus and Thisby would whisper secretly.

'Would you desire a wall to speak better?' Duke Theseus enquired of his fellow watchers, approvingly.

They hushed, as Pyramus crept in, soft-footed, and with much staring gloomily about him to ensure there was no doubt he came in *dangerous* secrecy.

'Oh grim-looked night! Oh night with hue so black!
Oh night which ever is when day is not!' he wailed.
'Oh wall, oh sweet lovely wall!
Show me thy chink, to blink through with mine eyes!'
Dutifully Wall held up two fingers.

'Thanks, courteous Wall,' said Bottom with tears of heartfelt gratitude in his eyes. He peered through the chink.

'But what see I? No Thisby do I see!' he rolled his eyes and clutched his heart.

'Oh wicked Wall!' he beat the Wall's sturdy breast (Wall staggered a little beneath the impassioned onslaught, but withstood it sturdily).

'I think the Wall being able to talk, should curse again.' Theseus whispered rather loudly to Hippolyta.

'No! In truth sir, he should not!' Bottom was most perturbed to find there was some confusion on this point. '"Deceiving me" is Thisby's cue,' he explained patiently to the confused Duke. 'She is to enter now and I am to spy her through the wall. You shall see . . . here she comes!'

Unfortunately for Bottom, Francis Flute was having a little trouble with his yellow wig. It would fly off whenever he tried to move. He clasped it firmly to his head and lolloped on, kicking the folds of his dress valiantly aside (though he had quite forgotten to change his boots).

Suddenly, and alarmingly, he was facing this distinguished audience. He peered owlishly at them, trembled with the seriousness of his forthcoming task, and squeaked determinedly.

'Oh Wall, my cherry lips have often kissed thy stones.'

'I see a voice,' gasped Pyramus, relieved to see his partner finally appear beyond the looming shape of Wall. 'Now will I to the chink!'

At this most poetic exclamation, the audience, who had been merely tittering, now dissolved in uncontrollable laughter.

'Oh kiss me through the hole of this vile wall,' shrieked Pyramus, now much enjoying himself and gathering momentum since the audience seemed to be having so much fun . . .

'I kiss the wall's hole, not your lips at all,' piped Thisby.

'Wilt thou at Ninny's tomb meet me straight away,' yelled Pyramus.

'I come without delay,' lisped Thisby from beneath the crooked wig, for it had now slid disconcertingly across one eye.

And out they marched, arm in arm, forgetting they were still two lovers separated by a wall . . .

Wall, left alone before a giggling audience, shuffled from foot to foot, summoned what remaining courage he had and belted out his lines at top speed.

'Thus have I, Wall, my part discharged, and being done, thus Wall away doth go!' and without further ado, he fled.

The audience waited expectantly. Lion came on (Snug's face peering reassuringly from beneath the shaggy head), and spoke a pretty speech to explain he was really Snug the joiner, and no fierce lion.

'A very gentle beast,' Duke Theseus approved, 'and of a good conscience.'

Now it was Moonshine's turn. Much encouraged by the loud noises emitting from the audience, he waved his lantern enthusiastically and yelled, 'This lantern presents the horned moon. Myself the man in the moon do seem to be!'

On cue, Thisby clumped in, saw the lion, who duly roared a mighty roar. Thisby ran off shrieking, then ran on again, propelled by Peter

Quince, to throw her cloak down on the ground. Lion seized the cloak, and with several lusty roars, tore it to shreds. Pyramus rushed on, saw the mangled cloak, assumed his lover Thisby dead, whipped out his sword, plunged it in his own breast, and fell moaning and grimacing with pain.

   'Now am I dead
   Now am I fled
   My soul is in the sky
   Tongue, lose thy light
   Moon take thy flight!'
   Though this last was not in the script as he remembered it,

Moonshine took Pyramus at his word, and galloped off.

Thisby, wig restored, rushed on.

'What, dead my dove?

Oh Pyramus, arise, speak, speak.

Quite dumb?

These lily lips, this cherry nose,

These yellow cowslip cheeks,' she intoned, warming greatly to the scene now that the play was nearly done.

And so the tragedy of Pyramus and Thisby galloped to its close, affording its audience no less transports of mirth and sheer delight than the antics of that same audience had once offered the sprightly Puck in that far-off, dream-washed, moonlit world outside the walls of Athens.

The palace was now quiet. The newly-weds had all retired to bed, wrapped in the magic of their love. And now a different magic came to touch Duke Theseus and his bride Hippolyta.

It was at first only a shimmering, and then a gentle whispering, a silver breeze that stirred across the halls, the kissing touch of shadows dancing with tinsel sounds across the moonbeams in the rooms . . . .

They came, the King of Fairies and his queen, with all their train of fairies, elves and sprites led by bright Puck, to bring their blessing to this house and all who slept in it . . .

Or was it no more than a moonlit dream from an enchanted midsummer night?

Much Ado About Nothing

It happened in Messina, beneath the deep blue of a Sicilian summer sky, where stately mansions clustered around the harbour, gazing out across the sea to catch a glimpse of distant mountain ridges in the toe of Italy. Signior Leonato was governor of the city, and busy in these long, hot days, with preparations for the entertainment of the Prince of Aragon and his companions. These gentlemen, high-ranking officers of the army, were on their way home from the wars. With the hardships of battle far behind them, their thoughts had turned, not unexpectedly, to relaxation and amusement and the joys of pleasant company . . .

And where better to find these than among old friends here in Messina, where the sun danced on the hills and fired the olive groves with light, and pleasant hours could be spent in graceful gardens laden with the scent of flowers . . .

There were two young gentlemen in particular, whose reputation preceded their arrival: one, Count Claudio of Florence, had in the recent wars surpassed all expectations of his bravery and skill; though he was young, it was said that he had, in the figure of a lamb, done the deeds of a lion . . .

There was also Signior Benedick of Padua, a young lord distinguished for another kind of bravery and skill, his audacity with words. With what lightning speed could Signior Benedick toss out a lively joke, leap to a quip, perform somersaults of conversation round his fellows, stabbing at them with affectionate mockery from which they barely recovered before his next assault.

Indeed, it was known that there was no one in Messina who could contend with Signior Benedick's rapier-thrusting wit . . . except, perhaps, for Beatrice, Signior Leonato's niece.

Beatrice and Benedick were old rivals. Between Beatrice and

Benedick there had long been a kind of merry war: they never met but there was a skirmish of wit between them. And though this tug-of-war was often jovial, it was also often tart and sharp; then each would retire, to nurse the wound inflicted by the other's tongue and plot the next assault . . .

As other women might wear dimples and blushes, Beatrice wore her humour. She brandished it with such vivacious confidence, such sparkling mirth that no one who knew her could remain long unaffected by her merriment.

Benedick was unaffected, or so he said. He scorned Beatrice as he scorned all women. And Beatrice derided Benedick as she derided all men: she had never yet met one who impressed her with anything other than his vanity . . .

In Messina Benedick and Claudio were much in each other's company, and it was to Benedick that Claudio admitted a new preoccupation since their arrival in that sunlit city. He had seen Leonato's daughter, Hero, again. Her modesty . . . her beauty like a jewel . . . the sweetest lady, he confessed to Benedick, that ever he looked on.

Benedick was unimpressed, being determinedly unimpressed, as always, with ladies of any kind; and he would be more unimpressed, he announced, if Claudio should contemplate tranforming himself from valiant soldier into husband. The much-praised delights of marriage were not delights that Benedick cared for . . . what was a marriage but a collar to thrust a man's head into and tie him up?

Claudio was used to Benedick's barbed wit, and was not listening. 'If Hero would be my wife . . .' he murmured, but wheeled round with some embarrassment at the arrival of the Prince of Aragon, Don Pedro, his patron and his friend.

But his confession could be kept no secret from Don Pedro, least of all with talkative Benedick about. In a trice he had spilled the story. 'He's in love!' Benedick announced with a flourish and an extravagant bow, mockery dancing across his face. 'With who? Mark how short his answer is: with Hero, Leonato's short daughter!'

Don Pedro approved, and clapped his young friend on the shoulder.

'The lady is very worthy,' he acknowledged.

'That I love her, I feel,' admitted Claudio, cautiously.

'That she is worthy, I know,' Don Pedro assured him, for clearly the young man needed encouragement to embrace his affection openly and marriage would not be a bad finale to his prowess in the wars.

But Benedick mocked their solemn discussion of a lady's worth.

Don Pedro wagged a finger at Benedick. 'Before I die, I shall see you look pale with love,' he warned, laughing.

'With anger, with sickness or with hunger, my lord, not with love,' vowed Benedick and went off gaily to take their greetings to the governor and confirm they would be able to attend his ball that night.

Without Benedick's teasing tongue to throw him off his quest, Claudio pursued the subject of Leonato's pretty daughter with Don Pedro, and it was not unexpected that his fascination grew on learning that the exquisite lady, being Leonato's only child, was therefore also the sole heir to old Leonato's fortune, which, if he married her, would all be his!

Don Pedro saw his young friend's heart was truly settling on this lady; he so much approved the match that he offered his own services to push the matter further . . . He suspected that young Claudio, though distinguished for his bravery in war, would not, in love, distinguish himself with any speed in approaching either the lady or the father. So Don Pedro himself would woo Hero for Claudio! And he would do it that very evening, at Leonato's ball.

He laid his plan out quickly: they would all be wearing masks; he would pretend to be Claudio and confess his love to Hero. If the lady's heart was won, he would at once seek Leonato's blessing, and so, swiftly, they could tie the marriage knot!

But in Messina with the prince there was also the prince's brother, Don John. Don John did not share his brother's mood of pleasure and release from the hardships of the war. Don John did not share any of his brother's pleasures, for Don John hated the prince, loathed all the prince's friends, and looked for any chance to cause him harm. He had rebelled against him, but had been defeated. He had been forgiven and was received again by Don Pedro into favour.

But this generosity had not bought Don Pedro either Don John's love or gratitude, or anything resembling a brother's loyalty. It only fed Don John's resentment so that his hatred grew, looking for a place to fasten its claws and tear . . .

He hated also, in particular, his brother's friend, Count Claudio, who had won glory from the overthrow of Don John's rebellion, and sat now, so comfortable in the glow of Don Pedro's gratitude.

So it was with malevolent pleasure that Don John discovered his brother's plan to woo Hero for Claudio. A villain named Borachio had overheard the prince and Claudio talking of it and was quick to recognize it's possible use for his unpleasant master . . .

Don John embraced the news with fervour: it would surely give him food for his displeasure, and provide the tool with which to avenge himself on up-start Claudio!

They gathered beneath the twinkling chandeliers in Leonato's house, and the rainbow colours of their finery rivalled the sumptuous tapestries and flowers, while plates piled high with crystallized fruits sparkled like jewels . . .

All of them were masked, so that the evening was one of tantalising, teasing mystery . . . Who was this elegant gentleman enticing Hero off to dance? And who the courtly fellow who whisked Margaret, Hero's gentlewoman away? And here was old Antonio, Leonato's brother, pretending not to be himself, though his discerning partner could tell by the waggling of his head . . .

And who was this couple sparring with each other, their words like

33

darting swordplay? The one was Beatrice and the other Benedick, though whether each recognized the other and did not admit it, or whether they truly did not know, was quite impossible to tell.

Beatrice was feeling a little snubbed: she had been told that Benedick belittled the quality of her wit, and now, stung to a defence, she launched her counter-attack.

'I am sure you know Benedick well enough,' she said.

'Who's he?' masked Benedick enquired, casually pretending he was not Benedick.

'Why,' Beatrice rejoined, ready to repay scorn with scorn. 'He is the prince's jester: a very dull fool, his only gift is in making up impossible slanders . . .'

Did she know that Benedick was her listener, Benedick wondered. Did she make this comment as a joke? Or was she ignorant whose face lurked behind the mask, and did she truly mean what she had said?

'When I know this gentleman, I'll tell him what you say,' he answered, and was a little cross that his reponse was lame: the sharp-tongued lady's words, if he was honest, had cut him to the quick. The prince's fool!

This description, complete with Beatrice's dismissive tones, would not leave Benedick's head again for the whole evening, though he would not, for all the world, have let his disdainful accuser guess . . .

That woman, Benedick was to tell Don Pedro later, could not be endured. Every word she said was like a dagger's stab . . . 'Oh sir,' he exclaimed, seeing the lady in question advancing towards them, 'here's a dish I love not: I cannot endure my Lady Tongue.' And he fled before the possibility of being stabbed further.

Meanwhile Don Pedro had kept his promise. He had pretended to be Claudio, confessed his love to Hero, and discovered an answering love in her. Losing no time, he had gone to find her father and obtain his blessing on a marriage between Hero and Count Claudio . . .

But such pleasant schemes were not the only plots being fostered in that ballroom on that sparkling summer night. Don John, the prince's melancholy brother, had arrived. With brooding, spiteful eyes, he watched his brother wooing Hero. He looked for Claudio, and found him anxiously awaiting the outcome of the prince's efforts. He drew near to him, and with an air of innocence, pretended he believed that Claudio was Benedick.

Claudio, true to the spirit of the ball, and having no suspicion of Don John's malicious motives, pretended that he was Benedick.

'Signior Benedick,' Don John went on, maintaining the pretence, 'you are very near my brother and his love; he loves Hero; I beg you, dissuade him from her, she is no equal for his birth . . .'

The prince loved Hero! This possibility had not occurred to Claudio before. He looked again at Hero, smiling at Don Pedro, and while a moment ago this scene had been only his friend wooing Hero for Claudio, it was instantly transformed into the unmistakable signs of Don Pedro wooing on his own behalf!

It never occurred to Claudio to wonder if the prince was capable of such dishonesty. Claudio believed appearances. He did not delve below the surfaces of things. He trusted only the outward show. And in his short, prosperous, successful life, he had no reason to learn otherwise.

So now he simply heard, saw, and believed. Don Pedro was wooing for himself! It seemed that friendship was constant in all things except in the affairs of love . . .

Don John watched the gullible youth with glee. Was it so quickly done? Was this much-praised, so-noble Claudio no more than a blank page on which the nearest man could write?

But, as Don John would swiftly find out, the writing could as easily be wiped away again . . .

'Here, Claudio,' Don Pedro's voice boomed triumphant in Claudio's ear. 'I have wooed her in your name, and fair Hero is won. I have told her father, and his good will is obtained. Name the day of marriage, and God give you joy!'

'Count, take my daughter,' Leonato confirmed these words, 'and with her take my fortunes.' Claudio was a most suitable husband for a daughter, young, handsome, of some repute, and wealthy . . .

As swiftly as it had come, all doubt vanished from Claudio's mind. Hero won! For him! A father's blessing on a prosperous marriage! He clasped her hand, most joyfully.

'Lady, as you are mine, I am yours: I give away myself for you and dote upon the exchange!'

'Speak, cousin,' Beatrice urged Hero, who stood blushing and glossy-eyed before the man that she would marry. 'Speak. Or if you cannot,' she laughed, seeing that look of enchantment still wrapping up her cousin's face, 'stop his mouth with a kiss, and let him not speak.'

Don Pedro looked at Beatrice appreciatively. 'In faith, lady, you have a merry heart,' he said.

Beatrice shook her head, mock sorrow on her face. 'Thus everyone gets married . . . and I may sit in a corner and cry heigh-ho for a husband!' and she sighed elaborately.

'Lady Beatrice, I will get you one,' Don Pedro declared, and bowed low before her. 'Will you have me, lady?'

'No, my lord,' retorted Beatrice, with a solemn curtsey, 'unless I might have another husband for working-days: your grace is too costly to wear every day . . .'

With amusement, Don Pedro watched her go. A pleasant spirited lady indeed, with whom many a witty hour could easily be spent! And, he had detected, a lady who would not seriously entertain thought of a husband. Leonato confirmed this: she was well known for her mockery of any man who tried to seek her hand in marriage!

Don Pedro's smile began to broaden. A fascinating scheme occurred to him, a scheme to while away the time most pleasantly while at Messina. This Beatrice who scorned husbands, would make an excellent wife for Benedick, who scorned wives!

'Oh Lord, my lord, if they were married for no more than a week, they would talk themselves mad,' Leonato laughed.

But Don Pedro had made up his mind. He would, in the time between now and Claudio's wedding to Hero a week away, strive to bring Signior Benedick and Lady Beatrice into a mountain of affection with each other. Leonato, Claudio and Hero must help him with it . . .

Don John's plan to foil Claudio's marriage had failed: he brooded now on other ways to kill this wedding.

Borachio never lacked ideas for villainous schemes: why not use Margaret, Hero's gentlewoman, to set up 'proof' of Hero's faithlessness? Margaret was in love with Borachio: she suspected nothing of his villainy. She could be persuaded to dress as Hero, and to stand at Hero's bedroom window, talking to Borachio. Meanwhile Don John would, in a tone of sorrowful discovery, 'reveal' the terrible news to Don Pedro and Count Claudio. He would 'reveal' that he had discovered Hero was not honourable, and that she entertained another lover even as she was about to marry Claudio. He would bring them to see the woman standing at the window in the dead of night, engaged in secret conversation with another man . . .

So would Don Pedro and Claudio 'see' clear proof of her unfaithfulness, so would the prince be duped, Count Claudio's prospects for a happy marriage ruined, Hero undone, and Leonato driven even to death by the shame of his daughter's guilt . . .

In Leonato's house, amongst family and guests alike, the days galloped joyfully towards the wedding.

Benedick, settling in the shady orchard to while away an afternoon in reading, began to muse instead on the strangeness of men's ways. 'Take Claudio, for example: I do much wonder that one man, seeing how much another man is a fool when he dedicates himself to love, will, after he has laughed at such shallow follies in others, become the object of his own scorn by falling in love!' He shook his head as a vision of Claudio rose before his eyes. Where was the plain-speaking, simple soldier now? Disappeared into a banquet of fancy clothes and courtly words! Benedick laughed. Such idiocy, and all in the name of love! Love would never make such a fool of Benedick!

He noticed suddenly that Don Pedro, Leonato, and Claudio had

entered the garden, and on an impulse he kept very quiet, hoping
perhaps to hear some choice titbits on the subject of love with which to
harass them later . . .

He did not see their elaborate pretence at not seeing him. He did not
hear the whispered conversation that they meant him not to hear. He
only heard the words most carefully designed for him, and they were
quite the most extraordinary remarks he had ever heard . . .

First, from Don Pedro. 'What was it you told me of today, Leonato,
that your niece Beatrice was in love with Signior Benedick?'

Benedick, lounging lazily along the arbour bench, sat bolt upright.

Then, from Claudio, who was much enjoying the part assigned to
him in the plot, stung as he was by Benedick's mockery of his love for
Hero. 'I never thought that lady would have loved any man.'

'No, nor I,' Leonato agreed, 'but it is most wonderful that she should
dote on Signior Benedick, whom she has seemed always to abhor!'

Benedick, still fretting at Beatrice's remark about a prince's jester,
was inclined to agree with this. But there was more . . .

'I cannot tell what to think of it, but that she loves him with a frenzied
affection,' Leonato was saying, having some difficulty keeping a straight
face.

'How, how,' Don Pedro pressed on. 'You amaze me: I would have
thought her spirit was invincible against all assaults of affection.'

'I would have sworn it was, my lord, especially against Benedick,'
Leonato agreed.

And listening, Benedick agreed, and would have thought the whole conversation was a trick to beat him with, except that old Leonato had spoken it, and surely Leonato was beyond such jesting?

'Has she made her affection known to Benedick?' enquired Don Pedro, solemnly.

'No.' Leonato sighed (most sorrowfully, it seemed to Benedick), 'and swears she never will: that's her torment. She has only told my daughter Hero, and she has just told me.'

Unfortunately, Benedick could hear no more; his friends, without a backward look, strolled on (though this took some effort of will, particularly from Claudio who was dying to see Benedick's face).

Benedick emerged from hiding. A trick? This could not be a trick. Their conversation was too serious. They had the truth of the whole matter straight from Hero's mouth, and who could know Beatrice better than her affectionate cousin and companion?

'Love me!' Benedick said the words with fascination. *Beatrice* love him! *Beatrice* suffering for him! The thought was so extraordinary . . .

Why, such suffering must be ended! Such love demanded to be answered! The thought was again so fascinating that in an instant it had captured him and held him prisoner. He heard again the judgements of Don Pedro and Claudio, that he would be harshly proud and cast the lady off. He searched, and found no tell-tale harshness, pride or scorn: instead a miraculous desire to answer the lady's love with love!

The next thought struck him like a thunder-clap. Marriage! 'I did never think to marry . . .' he assured himself, as though giving witness in a court, but, there it was, unmistakable, in his head. 'I must not seem proud,' he resolved. Truly, the lady was fair, and virtuous, and wise. And admitting it like this, it was a knowledge he had always had.

'I will be horribly in love with her,' he declared to the world, if any of the world were lurking in that sunlit orchard. Though it occurred to him as well that he would undoubtedly suffer the remnants of her sarcastic wit: he had argued for too long against marriage to escape punishment from her for falling from this stance.

But (he was drawing closer to his verdict now), well, a man's appetite must change . . . a man loves the meat in his youth that he cannot endure in his old age.

'The world must be peopled.' He announced this with a sense of having scaled a mountain and reached a judgement of significance to all

39

the human race. 'When I said I would die a bachelor, I did not think I would live till I was married,' and having thus most satisfactorily excused (to himself at least) this remarkable transformation from the enemy of all romantic love to a man contemplating imminent marriage, he was transfixed by the arrival, in the orchard, of Beatrice!

She had been sent by Don Pedro and Leonato to fetch Benedick to dinner, for these plotters could hardly wait to find out if the fish had seized the bait.

Benedick's first thought on seeing her, unlike any thought he had ever had before about Beatrice, was that she was, without question, most beautiful! His second, was that there were some distinct marks of pining love about her . . .

Beatrice, who was quite innocent of any such emotions, and unaware of all the little scenes concerning her which had so occupied that sunny afternoon, had come most reluctantly to find him.

Her own transformation was already being plotted, and so it was that before the day was out, she too was overhearing conversations in that orchard. 'But are you sure, that Benedick loves Beatrice so entirely?' one of Hero's gentlewomen, Ursula, was asking.

'So says the prince, and my newly betrothed lord, Claudio,' Hero assured her. 'They begged me to tell her of it. But I persuaded them, if they loved Benedick, to wish that he would wrestle with his love, and never let Beatrice know of it.' She turned away from Beatrice, hiding in the honeysuckle, in case her cousin's sharp eyes should detect the laughter quivering on her lips . . .

'But Nature never framed a woman's heart of prouder stuff than that of Beatrice,' Hero told Ursula, 'disdain and scorn ride sparkling in her eyes! She cannot love . . .' And then to draw their quarry closer to the bait, they painted a portrait of Benedick's rare virtues: what a husband he would make: a gentleman, known for his valour, behaviour and good name, an excellent wit . . .

Having to their satisfaction laid the snare, the two merry plotters disappeared, barely controlling their mirth till they were out of sight.

And Beatrice, abandoned suddenly in the balmy evening light, was caught in the grips of a most extraordinary inner glow.

'What fire is in my ears?' she whispered. Could what she had heard be true? Was she condemned for pride and scorn so much?

She searched her heart, as Benedick had done, and felt no pride or scorn in it. But there *was* something else . . .

'Benedick, love on,' she cried suddenly, for in her heart of hearts there was a picture stirring: Beatrice with her wild heart tamed by a loving Benedick's hand: *Benedick and Beatrice, wed!*

Benedick was transformed. He complained mournfully of the toothache (the commonest plague of lovers, it was said) and according to Claudio, he had been seen to brush his hat in the morning, was newly shaved, and could be sniffed out by the aroma of fashionable perfume that floated around him. More to the point, Don Pedro noted, he had that unmistakable air of a lover's melancholy.

Benedick was, for once, no match for all this mockery.

'The sweet youth's in love!' teased Claudio.

'Conclude, conclude he is in love,' Don Pedro echoed.

'This is no charm for the toothache,' moaned Benedick, and wandered off . . .

Claudio's jollity was spiced with more than the simple pleasure at Benedick's plunge into romance. On the following day, Claudio would marry Hero. The days they had spent in her company had only heightened his expectations of this marriage. Excitement, anticipation, most wonderful, overflowing love had filled his heart . . .

So he was unprepared for the arrival of Don Pedro's brother, Don John. The villain's show of 'grief', his ominous questions, took the eager bridegroom quite by storm. Though at first he did not understand . . .

'The lady is disloyal,' Don John was saying.

'Who, Hero?' Claudio asked, confused.

'Even she: Leonato's Hero, your Hero,' nodded Don John, and paused, 'every man's Hero.'

'Disloyal?' repeated Claudio.

'The word is too good to paint out her wickedness,' Don John murmured sadly. But with what inner glee he saw that Count Claudio was already swallowing the bait! No hesitation, no angry refusal to believe, no accusations of false slander against his bride to be! Instead, a look of hurt, that became horror, and then disgust that he could be so cheated by one he thought so fair . . .

They could, Don John told them, see her in the very act of

faithlessness, now, on the night before her wedding!

'I will not think it,' Don Pedro protested.

'If you will follow me, I will show you enough,' Don John assured him, 'and when you have seen more and heard more, proceed.'

'Disloyal' echoed menacingly in Claudio's mind. Hero did not love him! She flourished her faithlessness for all to see! He did not search his heart for what he knew of her (and if the truth were told, he knew little, except that she was beautiful and merry company). Nor did he remember that he had once before been given a false report by this same man, concerning the prince and Hero . . .

He simply felt these accusations like a stab-wound to his love, his dignity, his pride – and in an instant his belief in Hero's innocence was gone. 'If I see anything tonight why I should not marry her tomorrow . . .' he muttered, 'in the congregation, where I should wed, there will I shame her.' And wearing his offended anger like a badge, he followed Don John into the streets to see the 'proof'.

Messina's streets that night were being watched. They were watched every night, but on this night the Master Constable Dogberry, and Verges, his lieutenant, had given most particular instructions to the constables of the Watch, and the constables of the Watch had tried, most earnestly, to listen. They were to take their lantern, Master Constable Dogberry instructed them, make no noise in the streets, ensure their weapons were not stolen and send all drunkards in the ale-houses to bed.

The Watch, taking careful note of these important orders, decided to sit upon the church-bench until two, and then all go to bed, a plan that would have been put swiftly to effect had not Constable Dogberry returned. He had one last instruction for the Watch: they were to watch most particularly around Signior Leonato's door, for there was a wedding there tomorrow, and a great bustle going on tonight . . .

And so it came about that Dogberry's reluctant watchmen stood by Leonato's door, and heard Don John's accomplice, Borachio, boasting to his friend. He had, he said, earned a fat reward from Don John for this night's work: he had visited Margaret, one of the Lady Hero's gentlewomen, and called her by the name of Hero. Margaret, dressed like Hero and leaning from Hero's bedroom window, answered with mirthful whispers, loving sighs and all the marks of secret love; Claudio and Don Pedro peering through the darkness at this scene, believed that she was the real Hero with a lover on the night before her wedding!

The Watch, though still hoping for a quiet night and early bed-time were honest men at heart, and on hearing such villainy they sprang to their duty and arrested Borachio and his friend for (as they declared vehemently), the most dangerous piece of lechery ever known . . .

The morning of the wedding dawned. Hero awoke, nursing a kind of wavering gloom she did not understand. But this anxiety was quickly put to flight by light-hearted banter from Margaret (whose happiness was heightened by the unexpected devotion of Borachio the night before) and by the arrival of Beatrice, most decidedly unlike her usual self! Unlike Benedick's tooth-ache, Beatrice insisted that she had a cold. But to the questing eyes of Margeret and Hero, her illness showed distinct signs of being more to do with a change of tune on the subject of men, love, marriage . . . and Benedick?

And already Ursula was bustling in to hurry them: the prince, Count Claudio, Benedick, Don John and all the gentlemen of the town had come to fetch the eager bride to church . . .

Elsewhere, in another part of Leonato's house, an interview was taking place. Master Constable Dogberry and his lieutenant Verges had come to impart important information to Governor Leonato. Indeed, their information was no less than vital to the events about to happen in the church, for these two honest officers of the law had come to inform Leonato about the plot they had discovered: the plot against the honour, reputation, and the marriage of his daughter, Hero.

The problem was that what Constable Dogberry and Verges *planned* to do, and what they actually did, were two quite different things. To begin with, some time was needed (particularly by Constable Dogberry) to display to Governor Leonato how serious, honest, earnest, and most knowledgeable they were, and though Verges made a valiant attempt to begin the tale of the two villains arrested during the night, his effort was eclipsed by the talkative Dogberry, for whom it was a welcome cue to point out, at length, his faithful lieutenant's worth . . .

By the time all this was done, Leonato was so anxious to be away to his daughter's wedding that he gave up any attempt at listening and hastily directed them to undertake interrogation of the arrested men themselves, and bring him their report of it . . . and off he rushed, hot-foot into Don John's snare.

All eyes were on the bride: Leonato's eyes of pride, Beatrice's eyes of warm affection (with an occasional stolen glance at Benedick), the Friar's eyes, shortly to read the marriage ceremony, aglow with happiness at this loving union between two people, and Benedick's eyes unusually dreamy, straying secretly towards Beatrice.

But other eyes watched Hero with different lights in them: Don John's were filled with malevolent anticipation, Don Pedro's with offended dignity, and Count Claudio's with an ugly gleam of vengeance.

'You come here, my lord,' the Friar began, 'to marry this lady.'

There was a ripple of delighted anticipation through the air . . . All eyes on Claudio.

'No,' said Claudio.

'To be married to her,' insisted Leonato, assuming there was some confusion. 'Friar, you come to marry her,' he urged.

The Friar began again. He turned to Hero. 'Lady, you come here to be married to this count,' he said.

'I do,' said Hero, and waited with pounding heart for Claudio to pledge his vow.

For answer, Claudio swung to look at Leonato, and the anger in his eyes was unmistakable. 'Will you with free and unconstrained soul, give me this maid, your daughter?' he asked, in haughty tones.

'As freely, son, as God did give her to me,' old Leonato answered.

'There, Leonato, take her back again,' Claudio's voice rang out. 'Give not this rotten orange to your friend! Her blush is guiltiness, not modesty!'

'What do you mean?' gasped Leonato, comprehending nothing. His ears took in the words, but not the meanings hurled at him: his daughter vile, faithless, worthless! Was this all a dream?

'This does not look like a wedding,' was all Benedick could say, amazed.

'What man was it that talked with you last night, out of your window, between twelve and one?' Claudio challenged Hero triumphantly.

'I talked with no man at that hour, my lord,' protested Hero, white with shock.

Don Pedro intervened. 'Leonato, I am sorry you must hear this;

44

upon my honour, myself, my brother and this grieved count did see her, hear her, at that hour last night, talk with a ruffian at her chamber window.' And even more: that same ruffian had confessed a thousand meetings of this kind with Hero, secretly . . .

'Most foul, most fair,' Claudio hurled at Hero. 'Farewell! I will lock up all the gates of love . . .'

Hero's face drained of all colour. She swayed, shuddered, and crumpled to the floor. Beatrice let out a cry and ran to her, suddenly afraid that she was dead.

Don Pedro and Count Claudio, smugly confident they had unmasked a most dishonest lady, marched from the church, their honour and their dignity (they thought) intact.

Old Leonato, thoroughly confused, and of long-standing opinion that princes and counts could never lie, stared at his innocent daughter, and saw in the unconscious girl only the evidence of guilt. Thus had she, on her wedding day, put the stamp of foul dishonour on herself, on him,

on the whole family; he promptly let out such a wail of misery at so many losses bound up all in one . . .

Beatrice, convinced at first that Hero had died of shock, had discovered that she was stirring. Her joy at finding her cousin still alive gave way at once to such a passion at the horror of what had happened here. *She* had no doubts of Hero's innocence. This was a foul slander on her cousin, lies . . .

The Friar, who was a wise, observant and cautious man, had watched the Lady Hero throughout the most extraordinary wedding ceremony he ever had the misfortune to begin. He had seen in her ashen face nothing but evidence of innocence, and so he told Leonato in plain, no-nonsense words, once he could make himself heard above that gentleman's laments.

But would the prince lie? Leonato could not believe he would! Would Claudio lie? Leonato did not believe he would! It could not be!

Benedick, who did not know what to think, but whose instincts had led him to stay and cast his lot on Hero's side, was of the opinion that the source of this mischief lay not in lies by Claudio or the prince, but somewhere with the villainous Don John who was always at the root of mischief . . .

Faced with such conviction of his daughter's innocence, Leonato's wailings began to waver. Hero, recovering from her faint, begged him to believe her innocence. Leonato began to wonder. And as he wondered, he began to wind the other way, growing angry, furious, mounting to rage against anyone who dared to tell a scurrilous lie about his daughter . . .

The Friar, whose head was ever cool, and might have told the father that these fighting words would have been more useful a little while ago, now had a plan to extricate them from their predicament: the prince and Claudio had marched away, leaving Hero in a faint, even dead, for all they knew. Their ignorance of what had happened after they had left, could be most useful . . .

Leonato must let it be known throughout Messina that Hero had died, in the church, from shock. The family must 'bury' her, and at her 'tomb' follow all rites of mourning for her loss . . . In this way, the Friar hoped the slanders would be transformed to sorrow, and that impetuous young man who had so easily cast her away, might learn remorse in hearing she had died upon his words . . .

So they agreed, and so they left the church: the rejected bride, the wounded father, and the hopeful Friar.

Benedick and Beatrice remained. They faced each other silently. This was the first meeting between the two, since both had 'learned' that the other loved them. This was the meeting that their plotting friends had hoped to witness, in happier times . . .

Benedick eyed Beatrice cautiously. He advanced a little closer.

'Surely, I do believe your fair cousin is wronged,' he said.

'Ah,' Beatrice cried passionately, 'how much would I give to the man who could prove her innocent!'

Benedick drew closer still. 'Is there any way to show such friendship?' He stood looking at her, wondering if he dared to tell her that he knew she loved him.

Instead the opposite confession tumbled out. 'I do love nothing in the world as well as you – is that not strange?' he murmured, wonderingly.

It was no stranger though than the confession which tumbled out of Beatrice, though not without some twisting and wrenching at it from determined Benedick. But now that it was out, she said it several times, liking the sound of it. 'I love you with so much of my heart that none is left to protest,' she said.

'Come, bid me do anything for you,' Benedick urged her, recklessly.

The passion of her anger for her cousin's plight, eclipsed for a moment by the music of these lovers' revelations, now returned, more violent than before. She looked at Benedick, and the sudden fury on her face was terrible. 'Kill Claudio,' she said.

'Ha! Not for the wide world,' Benedick retorted, shocked to have his offer taken up like this.

'You kill me to deny it,' Beatrice cried out. 'Is he not a villain that has slandered, scorned, dishonoured my kinswoman? What, say nothing until they come to the church, and then with public accusation . . .'
Her indignation overcame her tongue and she could go no further. She turned on her heel to stride away from him.

'But Beatrice,' Benedick attempted to dissuade her.

'Sweet Hero,' she cried. 'She is wronged! She is slandered! She is undone!'

'Beat . . .' Benedick tried to intervene again, in vain.

'Princes and counts!' snorted Beatrice. 'Surely a princely testimony, a goodly count!'

It was finally enough for Benedick. 'Do you think in your soul that Count Claudio has lied about Hero?' he challenged her.

'As sure as I have a thought or a soul,' declared Beatrice fiercely.

'Enough,' declared Benedick. 'I will challenge him!' He took a long, lingering gaze at her. 'I will kiss your hand, and so I leave you.' But having gained possession of her hand, he lingered, and the moment stretched . . . 'Go,' he said finally, 'comfort your cousin . . .'

But even as they put the Friar's plan into effect and spread the news of Hero's tragic death, other help was near at hand, and from an unexpected quarter. Master Constable Dogberry and Verges had taken Governor Leonato at his word and questioned the arrested villains, Borachio and his friend. They had, therefore, proceeded towards the story (though with some twists and turns and not a few circles), with much laborious writing of the evidence, and a lot of talking in between, particularly from Constable Dogberry . . .

Aided finally by evidence from the Watch (who could have told them the whole story anyway, had anyone thought to ask them), finally the villainous tale came out. And so, as news of Hero's death broke upon the citizens of Messina, Dogberry and Verges could be seen bustling importantly towards Leonato's house . . .

Leonato knew nothing of his imminent rescue by these valiant custodians of law and order. He grieved for the slanders against Hero. He ached with sorrow. He burned for vengeance. Now utterly convinced of Hero's innocence, why then the prince and Claudio must be guilty! He grew hopping mad, and danced around them, despite his age, challenging them to a trial with swords; he hurled his daughter's death at Claudio as though it were a weapon (almost forgetting in his passion that she was not really dead).

These two, offended prince and cheated bridegroom, still had not an ounce of uncertainty about their accusation, summary trial and judgement in the church. It never occurred to them they might be wrong. This exotic behaviour by the old man was beyond their comprehension, as was the grim face and accusing looks from Benedick. Try as they might, they could not deflect him with any jest about his wit, his love, or what Beatrice had last said. He was angry, and *serious* about a challenge to a duel in defence of Hero's honour!

But help was bumbling towards them all. Help was entering the house. Help was finally here, in the unlikely shape of Dogberry, Verges, and the Watch with skulking Borachio and friend in tow.

And so it all came out. 'What your wisdoms could not discover, these shallow fools have brought to light,' Borachio said. 'The lady is dead upon mine and my master's false accusation . . .'

Don Pedro's face was white. Claudio's was whiter still.

A picture leapt before his eyes, of Hero as he had loved her first. And for the first time since he had heard Don John's poisonous words, he stopped, and looked at himself, and saw the mistake that he had made, and worse, how he had rushed to injure Hero without a moment's pause or thought, remorse or sorrow . . .

'I am guilty of her death – choose your revenge yourself,' Claudio cried to Leonato.

Leonato had already chosen it. He had a niece, he said, who looked so like dead Hero that she was almost a copy of her. If Claudio would

marry her, as he should have married Hero, then old Leonato would rest content.

And so it was agreed. Claudio, earnestly regretting his mistakes, did solemn and grieving penance at Hero's 'tomb' that night, and swore to do the same each year.

And then he went to bind himself in penance further to the unknown niece of Leonato.

At Leonato's house all grief had given way to mirth, and there was much bustling about in preparation for a wedding. But all the ladies now wore masks, and young Claudio would never see the one he married till the bonds were tied . . .

And so the good, wise Friar performed his wedding ceremony after all, and married Claudio to a veiled bride. True to his word, Claudio pledged himself to her, though he was much preoccupied with trying to see his new bride's face.

And when he did, what joy! Hero! Not dead! Alive! His bride!

And so, in the ecstasy of relief, all was forgiven and forgotten, and the young people's joy eclipsed the villainy of Don John and Borachio who had both fled for their lives . . .

And on that day there was a second bride. Finally, Beatrice married Benedick, though she swore it was only to save his life, for she had been told that he was dying, and Benedick swore that he loved her against his will and took her only in pity . . .

Twelfth Night

Duke Orsino was in love. Love perfumed the air with flowers, coloured the hills and cliffs with rosy light, filled the rooms in which Orsino roamed with wistful songs, their lilting notes drifting from palace balconies into the summer air.

'If music be the food of love, play on; give me excess of it,' he murmured to the strains of mournful melodies. He listened to a dying fall of notes. 'Oh, it came over my ear like the sweet sound that breathes upon a bank of violets . . .'

The duke lived for love, and dreamed of love, and sighed for love's melancholy. Indeed, if Duke Orsino's servants were to admit it (which they would not), the duke was truly in love with love itself, though he believed that the object of his adoration was a youthful and most beautiful countess named Lady Olivia.

Unfortunately for Duke Orsino, Lady Olivia did not love him. She would not love him: she could not love him: this was her only answer to his proffered love. She could love no man, for she had vowed to mourn her brother's death behind a veil, shedding tears for him in seven long years of sorrow. Since her brother's death she had allowed no visitors, no company of men near her, nor would she until the end of mourning.

And so Duke Orsino languished for love of Lady Olivia, and Lady Olivia languished for love of her dead brother, until one day, there came a stranger to that prosperous land of fair Illyria . . . Wild winds and towering waves off Illyria's rocky coast had plucked a passing ship and tossed it like a toy, spilling its passengers into the foaming waves to drift like flotsam and jetsam towards the shore.

As the storm had calmed, it threw them on the rocks, battered, drenched and exhausted by their battle with the sea, but nonetheless alive. But this was little comfort for the stranger, a young girl named

Viola. Somewhere in that storm-tossed sea her twin brother, Sebastian had also been fighting for his life, and Sebastian was dearer to her than any other person in the world.

Was he dead? Or was it possible that he survived as she had? She begged the good sea captain flung ashore with her: could Sebastian be alive? The captain gave her hope: after their ship had splintered he had seen Sebastian bind himself to a mast still floating on the sea, and there he was when last the captain saw him.

'For saying so, there's gold!' Viola cried, her eyes alight with renewed hope.

But now she shivered, though the winds had softened and the air was growing warm again. What was she to do now? Here was a country she did not know, and she a woman, quite alone in it . . .

The captain saw how the young girl's fears were growing again and tried to calm them. This Illyria was a prosperous, friendly, pleasant land. He knew it well, for he had been born and bred not three hours travel from this very place. And it was ruled well by a most noble, gentle duke, Orsino.

'Orsino!' Viola said. 'I have heard my father speak of him. He was unmarried then.'

And so was he now, the captain said, though there was talk among the people that he sought the love of the lady Olivia, who mourned her brother's recent death.

Already Viola had seen a possible escape from her predicament, for though her mind was much clouded with fears for her brother's life, she had quick wits and buoyant spirits to give her strength . . . She would have liked most to serve Olivia, for it seemed that this lady might be a partner in mourning a dead brother. But the sea captain was certain she would not be accepted as a servant at Olivia's house. Olivia admitted no one.

Yet might it not be possible to obtain a position at Duke Orsino's court? Quickly she enlisted the kindly captain's help: he must lend her clothes to disguise herself as a man. She would present herself as a page at the palace of Duke Orsino of Illyria!

'I'll serve this duke!' declared Viola. 'I can sing and speak to him in many sorts of music . . .' enthusiasm for this plan began to revive her spirits and she set off with the captain, happy to have some purpose to lift her thoughts from the persistent terrors for her brother's life.

Was he dead? The thought rose again. She pushed it back. On, on, to her disguise . . . She would become Duke Orsino's page, and trust to time and hope. Only this good sea captain would know her true identity . . .

Viola's plan worked better than her wildest dreams. The grace and delicacy of her woman's shape was hidden beneath the clothes of a young man, her long fair hair tight-curled beneath a cap; and so this pretty girl was transformed into a handsome youth whose smooth, unbearded face and light voice only made the Duke Orsino think that his new page was young, not yet having reached the age of manhood.

Viola, who in her page's disguise called herself Cesario, endeared herself to the love-sick duke with quite remarkable speed. The duke was quick to find that the 'young man' had an attentive ear and understanding eye. Within three days, 'Cesario' had heard the full history of Orsino's love for Olivia: each sigh, each loving message, each miserable rejection had been catalogued by the unhappy duke for his young page, as had the beauty, wisdom and glory of the object of his adoration, the fair Olivia.

Now Orsino asked Cesario to take up his pleas with Olivia, to be his, Orsino's, tongue to her, and carry his messages of love.

Viola listened to the tale with a heart throbbing with more than sympathy. She watched the duke's agony of unrequited love as though it was her own. Indeed, it almost could have been, for beneath her boy's clothes, Viola, Orsino's faithful page 'Cesario', was herself suffering the pangs of unrequited love. Within three days, Viola had fallen fathoms deep in love with Duke Orsino!

And now the agony grew worse. Orsino was asking her to carry his love messages to Olivia who scorned his love – the love that she, Viola would give anything to possess!

Well, she would take his messages, because of her own loyalty to the duke and (though she scarce admitted it) also because she was a little curious to find out more about Olivia.

Sir Toby Belch was as full of wind and good cheer as was his name. He was a large, rotund, jovial sort of man who's only aim in life was to consume as much food and drink as his enormous bulk could hold (preferably food and drink that others had paid for); and to do so with as much rollicking good fun, songs, games, and the exchange of wit as could be crammed into the time between getting up (recovering from being drunk), and going to bed, drunk and sated with good food.

Not content merely with his own carousing to disturb the gloom of mourning in Olivia's house, Sir Toby had seen fit to introduce another: one Sir Andrew Aguecheek, a gentleman as long and thin and pale as Sir Toby was round and plump and red. Nevertheless Sir Andrew was an excellent companion for Sir Toby, for though his brain was on the meagre side, his purse was deliciously robust and fat. More to the point, his purse was at the disposal of Sir Toby.

Sir Toby had devised a plan to keep himself in drink and food for as long as he had appetite to consume them and the strength to open his mouth. Olivia was to be persuaded to marry Sir Andrew Aguecheek. This was the general line of strategy, and for the moment the tactics required that the long, thin knight should hang about the house with Sir Toby on the chance of seeing Olivia. The more Sir Andrew hung about, the more time he had to while away; the more time he had to while away, the more money he must spend; the more money he spent, the more Sir Toby made himself jovially available to share it, to keep the hopeful suitor's spirits up, to exchange a song, a dance, a joke with him . . . and generally while away the days, weeks or months . . . as chance would have it.

For a place of sombre mourning, Olivia's house indeed contained a motley collection of souls: besides the undaunted Sir Toby and the aging Andrew Aguecheek, there was also Feste, Olivia's court jester, who had a tendency to wander off on business of his own whenever the fancy took him, and who therefore also felt the sting of maid Maria's warning tongue.

'My lady will hang you for your absence!' she chided him. 'Make your excuses wisely . . .!'

And indeed, when Olivia entered, dressed head to foot in black, accompanied by the sombre shadow of her steward, Malvolio, her face solemnly composed in that grieving look it had worn since her brother died, she was angry, seeing Feste.

'Take the Fool away,' she said, with a dismissive toss of her elegant head.

The Fool had quickly shaken out his wits and got them ready for fooling. He pulled his face into a mockery of her solemnity and mimicked that tossing head.

'Do you hear fellows? Take away the lady,' he declared.

'Sir,' protested Olivia, her solemn face giving way to the temptation of a smile despite herself, 'I told them to take *you* away.'

'Give me leave,' said the Fool, catching that fleeting glimmer of mirth and determined to prise it out so that his misdemeanours would be quite forgotten by Olivia, 'Give me leave to prove *you* a fool.'

'Can you do it?' asked Olivia, curious, for she had most decidedly foresworn all merriment.

'Good madonna, why do you mourn?' enquired the Fool, with mock solemnity.

'Good Fool, for my brother's death,' said Olivia, irritated to be so unfeelingly reminded of her grief.

'I think his soul is in hell, madonna,' announced the Fool.

'I know his soul is in heaven, Fool,' retorted Olivia.

'The more fool you, madonna, to mourn for your brother's soul being in heaven. Take away the fool!'

Despite her determination not to, Olivia laughed. She turned to Malvolio,

'What do you think of this Fool, Malvolio? Does he not improve?'

Malvolio, it must be said, disapproved. What, precisely, it was that Malvolio disapproved of, would be difficult to say, for Malvolio's sharp nose was tilted in the air at everything and everyone he saw, his nostrils flared as though a most unpleasant smell was caught beneath them, his lips pressed hard together with an air of pained endurance, and his eyes half-closed as though it were pure agony to waste their light on mortals such as these . . .

'I marvel your ladyship takes delight in such a barren rascal,' he intoned with a disdainful look towards Feste. 'I saw him put down the other day with an ordinary fool that has no more brain than a stone . . .'

'Oh, you are sick of self-love Malvolio,' Olivia interrupted him, laughing at him now. 'You taste with a sick appetite . . .'

She paused: the sound of raised voices had reached them, above all the boisterous tones of Sir Toby Belch.

Maria hurried in. There was, it seemed, a young gentleman at the gate determined to speak to Olivia.

Olivia sighed. Most probably another messenger from Orsino. She despatched Maria to rescue the messenger from Sir Toby's hospitality, for she could be fairly certain her uncle would be spouting drunken idiocies, and sent Malvolio to turn the messenger away. Any excuse would do, she was ill or not at home, anything, to rid her of this unwelcome intrusion.

It seemed, however, that not even Malvolio's disdainful nose could block the persistent young man. He was, it seemed, fortified against any denial.

Curious despite herself, Olivia enquired, 'What kind of man is he?'

'Why, of mankind,' Malvolio assured her pompously.

Olivia tried again. 'What does he look like? How old is he?'

Malvolio considered this question with some care, pursing his lips and flaring his nostrils with the effort of considering the possible worth of such a person in Malvolio's ranks of men . . .

'Not yet old enough for a man, nor young enough for a boy,' he announced. 'As an unripe peapod before it is a . . . peapod,' he continued, 'or an unripe apple when it is almost an apple. It is, with him, like at the turn of the tide, between boy and man . . .'

Malvolio had quite lost himself in the intricacies of these poetic images . . . Olivia gave up. And then, more from boredom than anything else, she succumbed to an unexpected curiosity. She would let this messenger in, just to have a look at him.

'Give me my veil,' she told Maria. 'Throw it over my face.'

Unaware of the stir he had created in this household so firmly barred against all visitors, the stranger marched in with a stride a little too consciously masterful and a voice a little too determinedly low; for the 'he' was not a he at all; it was a she . . . It was Viola, disguised as Cesario, the love-sick duke's new page.

Faced suddenly with *two* unknown young women, Viola paused and stared from one to the other.

'The honourable lady of the house, which is she?' she asked.

'Speak to me; I shall answer for her,' Olivia murmured from behind the veil. But though her tone suggested she was but slightly interested, a peep behind that lacy mask would have revealed another tale. Lady Olivia, mourning or otherwise, was not immune to the charms of so handsome a young man as this 'gentleman' who stood before her now.

Viola drew a deep breath and unfolded the paper on which she had written her speech. She was determined to discharge her task for her beloved duke as faithfully as she was able.

'Most radiant, exquisite and unmatchable beauty,' she began in ringing tones, but hearing a smothered titter from Maria, she halted. She looked from Maria to the veiled lady reclining gracefully on a chair.

'I pray you, tell me if this be the lady of the house, for I never saw her,' she said to Maria. 'I would be loathe to cast away my speech, for besides being excellently written, I have taken great pains to learn it.'

'Where do you come from sir?' enquired Olivia haughtily, intrigued against her better judgement by this earnest, though somewhat cheeky, persistence.

'I can say little more than I have studied,' protested Viola. She was frustrated by her inability to get on with the task in hand and return as fast as possible to Duke Orsino's side. 'Are you the lady of the house?'

And to be truthful, she was feeling rather angry. Here was this beautiful woman supposedly in mourning, yet behaving with an unseemly coquettish tilt to her graceful head, and apparently playing games with her, while Duke Orsino languished in misery for want of love.

'Speak,' sighed Olivia, seeing now that this young man could not be turned from his declared purpose.

Viola took a deep breath and launched, 'Most sweet lady . . .'

But two more interruptions from Olivia, and Viola saw that no suit from Duke Orsino would ever penetrate this woman's heart. She stared at her in miserable disbelief. Here was a woman who had the hand and heart of Duke Orsino for the asking, yet she spurned it. What was she like, this lady made of stone?

'Good madam,' she said suddenly, growing bold, 'let me see your face.'

'Have you a mission from your lord to negotiate with my face?' Olivia enquired softly. But the request had pleased her, for this youth (or so she thought he was) absorbed her more and more with every passing minute that he stood there earnest, honest, protesting for his lord.

'But we will draw the curtain and show you the picture,' she said. Slowly, she lifted the veil and showed her exquisite face. 'Is it not well done?' she enquired, with a gleam of mockery in her dark eyes.

'Excellently done . . . if God did all,' murmured Viola, at the same time admiring the flawless beauty displayed before her, and with a woman's discerning (and perhaps a little jealous) eye, searching for the touches of artistry that might give a bloom to cheeks and lips . . .

'It will endure wind and weather,' Olivia assured her, aware only that her face had made some impression on this handsome youth, and interpreting it as the palpitations of a beating heart much like that thundering in her own chest now.

'It is true beauty,' murmured Viola, searching the face Orsino loved so passionately. She saw the arch looks and the saucy smiles being thrown towards her; her sorrow for the scorned duke and for herself, prevented by her disguise from ever seeking Orsino's love, sent a hot flush of anger to her cheeks.

'If I did love you with my master's flame, with such a suffering, such a deadly life, I would find no sense in your denial; I would not understand it,' she pleaded.

'What would you do?' Olivia whispered, her eyes fixed on the youth's face. It seemed to have grown more handsome than ever before as he spoke again of his master's love.

'I would make me a willow cabin at your gate, and call upon my soul within the house; write songs of love and sing them even in the dead of night; cry out your name to the echoing hills and make the whispers of the air murmur 'Olivia'! Oh, you should not rest between the elements of air and earth, but you should pity me!'

For a long moment, Olivia sat looking at Viola's passionate face. It was as though her eyes were fastened by some magic to this youth and would never leave again.

Then she realized the look of fascination that must be showing on her face, and she dropped her eyes hurriedly, her cheeks colouring with sudden shame.

'You might do much,' she said, slowly, but she was talking to herself; for while the past half hour had started as a game, in boredom, and had continued as a tantalising teasing of this youth, it had become now something else. Olivia was listening to echoes within her heart that she had never heard before, echoes that she had vowed she would never hear till seven long years of mourning had gone by, echoes that she had believed she could not hear, for misery at her beloved brother's death.

This youth, entering her life merely as another's messenger, seemed to carry messages of another sort which tapped these slumbering echoes . . .

She tried to gather her composure. 'Get you to your lord,' she murmured, quietly now. 'I cannot love him; let him send no more . . .'

And then a sudden flare of daring took her again, and almost before she had realized what she said, she added hastily, 'Unless, perhaps, *you* come to me again . . . to tell me how he takes it. Fare you well.'

Behind the departing Viola's back, Olivia sat for a moment without moving. She could hear nothing but her thundering heart, feel nothing but the hot flush flooding her cheeks, see nothing but the vision of that handsome face ingrained for ever on her memory.

Almost before she knew what she was doing, she called Malvolio to her, pulling her ring off her finger, and holding it out to him.

'Run after that same peevish messenger, the duke's man,' she said, with a feigned air of carelessness. 'He left this ring behind.' She almost blushed at the lie, but Malvolio's nose had risen so high in the air at the sight of the disdained ring, that he was unaware of any tell-tale colours on his mistress's cheek.

'Tell him I'll have none of it,' ended Olivia hastily. 'Tell him not to flatter his lord, nor hold him up with hopes of my love; I am not for him; and,' she turned away, lest even Malvolio should see the flush rising across her face, 'if that youth will come this way tomorrow, I'll give him reasons for it.'

Nursing the ring gingerly as though it reeked of the scorned suitor, Malvolio marched out to do his mistress's will . . .

Two men were striding along a footpath that crossed a rocky headland. One, the elder, was speaking warmly, urgently to the younger man who seemed to shake his head and plead a little with his companion . . .

To the observer who had just seen Viola dressed as Cesario march angrily from Olivia's house, the sight of what appeared to be Cesario here, high on a rocky headland on the other side of Illyria, would have caused more than a little confusion.

At closer glance, the observer might have noticed that Cesario had changed his clothes and was not wearing the finery of a duke's page, that his face was somewhat squarer, giving the appearance of being larger, and that he did not wear a cap. (No one had ever yet seen Cesario without his cap, for the simple reason that without his cap, Cesario would have betrayed the rich tresses of a girl's fair hair.)

This Cesario had short-cropped hair, and was altogether broader, his frame much squarer . . .

And this was hardly surprising, for this was not Cesario, Viola disguised as Orsino's page. This was her brother, her twin, Sebastian whom she believed was dead, a youth so like his sister that they were almost two peas in the same pod that had so preoccupied Malvolio . . .

Shortly after his sister had safely reached the shore, Sebastian had been pulled from the waves by Antonio, the man who walked beside him now, protesting.

Their argument was simple: Antonio had grown to love this youth whose life he'd saved. He wanted Sebastian to stay.

Sebastian, on the other hand, was all for moving on. He was filled with gratitude and affection for Antonio's kindness, but he was also too well aware of how his sorrows for his sister (for he believed that she was dead), would make him always a burden to this kind man. His intention was to travel on, as fancy took him. If he stayed, tears and misery would constantly overwhelm him and he did not wish to impose his unhappiness on Antonio.

He had decided he would visit Duke Orsino's court, to see what time and fate might offer . . .

Antonio was a sea-faring man and had, in past sea-battles with Orsino's fleet, made enemies at Orsino's Court: going there would be unsafe for him. Yet watching Sebastian stride away, his love for the impetuous youth was stronger than any fears for his own safety . . . He threw all care to the winds and set off to keep Sebastian company, wherever his adventures might take him.

Viola knew nothing of her brother's miraculous presence in this land. She knew only that misery seemed to grow around her by the minute. Not only was she mourning a brother's death, but she was compelled to love a man who neither loved her, nor even knew she was a woman! She was compelled to carry messages of *his* love to another woman! And this woman was as hard-hearted as she was beautiful.

Now, to crown the sorry tale, here was that same Olivia's steward pursuing her from the house, his thumb and forefinger pinched together, disdainfully holding out a ring as if it were tainted with some unmentionable disease. And now he informed her that Olivia 'returned' the ring!

'If it be worth stooping for, there it lies . . . if not, let it be his that finds it,' intoned Malvolio, opening his fingers and letting the offending jewel drop to the ground. It rolled in a circle and stopped at Viola's feet. Malvolio swung on his heel and swept away.

Viola stared at the ring. 'I left no ring with her: what does this lady mean?'

But even as Malvolio disappeared from sight an awful thought entered Viola's brain. She bent down and picked up Olivia's ring. She held it cautiously in the palm of her hand. Could this be intended as a love token? Could her appearance, her *disguised* appearance, have charmed the lady into loving her, believing her to be a man?

The appalling thought was more awful than her wildest nightmares: 'My master loves her dearly; and I love him as much; and she, mistaken, seems to dote on me!' She pondered this circle of misery with dismay. 'What will become of this?' As long as she pretended to be a man, she would remain desperate for her master's love; yet as she was truly a woman, how many purposeless sighs would poor Olivia have to breathe for love of that non-existent youth, Cesario!

'Oh, time,' sighed Viola despairingly, 'you must untangle this, not I. It is too hard a knot for me to untie.'

Sir Toby Belch was in fine form. It was long past midnight: quantities of wine and most delicious food had been consumed, and still more was to be had; and he began to thump a rhythm with his boot and tankard, while Sir Andrew Aguecheek trilled merrily after him, and Feste the jester's considerably more musical tones rounded the whole thing off into the most jovial of uproars.

The rest of the household, sensibly fast asleep, could not remain so for long. Maria was the first to appear, hastily pulling on her dressing-gown.

'What a caterwauling do you keep here!' she cried. 'If my lady has not called up her steward Malvolio and bid him turn you out of doors, never trust me!'

For answer, Sir Toby seized the irate maid by the waist and waltzed her to and fro.

'O, the twelfth day of December . . .' he carolled.

'For the love of God, peace!' pleaded Maria, half-laughing now. And then she stopped.

An apparition was at the door. A long white nightgown, crowned by a long white nightcap which in turn framed a long white face crumpled with such disdain, disgust and horror that it must surely cripple any man for life to be so burdened with it.

It was Malvolio. He halted. He surveyed the assembled company. He allowed his eyes to come to rest finally, reluctantly, on Sir Toby Belch.

'My masters, are you mad or what are you?' he enquired in a voice shrill with affronted anger. 'Have you no wit, manners, nor honesty, but to gabble like tinkers at this time of night? Is there no respect of place, persons, nor time in you?'

'We did keep time, sir, in our songs,' retorted Sir Toby, and he thumped his knee in pleasure at this last fine gem of wit.

'Sir Toby,' shrieked Malvolio in rage. 'My lady bid me tell you that, though she harbours you as her kinsman, she's not attached to your misbehaviour. If you can separate yourself and your behaviour, you are welcome to the house; if not, she is willing to bid you farewell.'

For answer Sir Toby burst forth into song, and was joined by Feste the jester, who paid no respects to any man, least of all to disgruntled

62

household stewards who disapproved . . .

'Do you think,' Sir Toby thrust his face so close to the offended steward that Malvolio was forced to step hastily back for fear of being stifled by the fumes of ale. 'Do you think that because *you* are virtuous, there shall be no more cakes and ale?'

Malvolio had no answer. With a look of pure hatred that engulfed them all, the steward strode out, his nose higher than ever, his night cap swinging like the bell of doom, and his voice muttering darkly that Lady Olivia would hear of this . . .

Had not Maria held Sir Toby back, the infuriated man might well have rolled after Malvolio and boxed his ears into oblivion, for in all the rumpus Sir Toby had heard nothing of Olivia's pleas for good behaviour in her house; he heard only the insolent, offensive, always disapproving tones of Malvolio, whose gloomy face and appalling vanity seemed to bring the only cloud onto Sir Toby's jovial horizon, but a cloud that was always there.

'Sweet Sir Toby, be patient for tonight,' urged Maria. She had come herself in irritation at the noise made by Sir Toby and his fellow revellers; but in an instant this had been transformed by Malvolio's sour face into a burning desire to teach the acid-tongued steward a lesson, to find some sweet revenge . . .

'Since the youth of the duke was with my lady, she is much disturbed,' she warned Sir Toby Belch. 'As for Monsieur Malvolio, leave him to me . . .'

Sir Toby saw that some plan was taking shape in her sharp brain. In gleeful anticipation, he wrapped his arms about her robust waist, and planted an exuberant kiss on both her cheeks.

With a laughing tap on his nose, Maria swung herself free, and clapped her hands for their attention. The plan was in her mind, perfect . . . 'I will drop in his way some obscure letters of love,' she told her attentive audience, 'where, by the colour of his beard, the shape of his leg, the manner of his walk, the expression of his eyes, forehead and complexion, he shall find himself most accurately described. I can write very like my lady, your niece . . .'

'Excellent! I smell a trick!' Sir Toby slapped his knee in pure delight.

'I have it in my nose too!' chortled Sir Andrew Aguecheek . . .

'And he shall think,' Toby's brain was far from slow, and in that instant he had seen Maria's brilliant device, 'he shall think, by the

letters you will drop, that they come from my niece and that she's in
love with him!' he bellowed in ecstasy at the thought of any temptation
to Malvolio's disgusting vanity.

'I will hide you two where he shall find the letter,' Maria assured
them. 'Observe what he makes of it!' She wagged her finger at the
drunken pair. 'For this night, to bed, and dream on the event!'

'Come, come, I'll go drink some sherry; it is too late to go to bed
now,' declared Sir Toby. He wrapped his arm around the swaying Sir
Andrew's shoulders. 'Come, knight! Come, knight!'

Duke Orsino was talking of love. 'If ever you love, in the sweet pangs of
it, remember me,' he told 'Cesario', whose attentive ear provided him
with greater comfort than he had ever had. Once more he had been

rejected by Olivia. Once more he languished in the misery of unrequited love.

Orsino looked searchingly at Viola, though he saw no more than the figure of his faithful page Cesario and not the face of a woman who adored him more with every minute that she spent by his side. 'Young though you are, your eye has strayed upon some person that it loves, has it not, boy?' he enquired, gently and with a fatherly expression in his eyes.

'A little,' admitted Viola.

'What kind of woman is it?' the duke enquired.

'Of your complexion,' Viola replied, with beating heart.

'She is not worth you, then,' the duke dismissed this. 'And how old?'

'About your age, my lord,' Viola whispered, and looked with scarcely disguised longing into his face . . .

Orsino, of course, did not see that tell-tale lustre in her eyes. His thoughts had moved again to Olivia, and poor Viola was once more to be no more than his messenger to that lady, carrying further statements of Orsino's undying love.

'But if she cannot love you, sir,' Viola protested, frustrated with this thankless task and distressed that she would be again the bearer of such hurtful news to this man that she adored.

' I cannot accept that answer,' Orsino pushed the thought away.

'But you must!' persisted Viola. 'Say that some lady, as perhaps there is,' she wondered if the flush colouring her cheeks could be seen by Duke Orsino, 'say that some lady has for your love as great a pang of heart as you have for Olivia: you cannot love her; you tell her so; must she not then be answered?'

'There is no woman's heart can hold the beating of so strong a passion as love gives to my heart,' cried the heart-sick duke. 'Make no comparison between the love a woman can bear me and that I owe Olivia!'

'Aye, but I know . . .' Viola burst out, in misery.

'What do you know?' enquired the duke.

Viola was so close to spilling out her love for him, that in a moment she would have plunged across the precipice. 'Too well what love women may bear for men,' she cried. 'My father had a daughter loved a man, as might be . . . perhaps, . . . were I a woman . . . I should love your lordship . . .'

65

The duke looked at his earnest page with some amusement. He put an arm about the young lad's shoulders, ' And what's her history?'

Viola lowered her eyes, afraid that he would see the light of love in them. 'A blank, my lord,' she murmured. 'She never told her love, but let concealment, like a worm in the bud, feed on her damask cheek: she pined in thought, and with a green and yellow melancholy she sat like patience on a monument, smiling at grief . . .'

And she smiled up at him, mistress of her unruly emotions once again. 'Was this not love indeed?'

'But did your sister die of her love, my boy?' the duke persisted, intrigued by this melancholy tale.

'I am all the daughters of my father's house . . .' whispered Viola almost lost again, and teetering on the brink of telling all . . . 'and all the brothers too . . .' she ended hastily. She turned from him, hastily composing her face as was more fitting for the servant of a noble duke. 'Sir, shall I to this lady?'

'Aye, that's the theme. To her in haste,' Orsino urged. 'Give her this jewel, say my love can give no place, waits no denial . . .'

The letter glinted, tantalising in the morning sun. Behind the exuberant blooms of a large flowering bush, three figures crouched, though there could be nothing secret about their presence there. Sir Toby chortled, Sir Andrew cackled, and Fabian, another of Olivia's servants, hissed and hushed at them both. To any other person walking in that sunlit garden, the dishevelled, boisterous trio would have been instantly visible.

But not to Malvolio. Malvolio was busy. Malvolio was deep in a most exquisite fantasy. Malvolio was not Malvolio, Olivia's servant, but Malvolio, a great and powerful nobleman . . . and Malvolio had been practising a nobleman's behaviour to his own shadow for the past half hour. Indeed Malvolio was quite lost in this inspiring vision of himself. He addressed the trees, the sky, the sun, and all were courtiers to him . . .

'To be Count Malvolio,' he said, rolling the words around his tongue, 'having been three months married to Olivia . . . calling my officers about me,' he waved a peremptory hand towards the trees, 'in my branched velvet gown, having come from a day-bed where I have left Olivia sleeping . . .'

'Fire and brimstone!' spluttered Sir Toby Belch, and nearly fell out of the bush. He was yanked back out of sight by Fabian.

'Telling them . . .' Malvolio smirked at the thought of this next vision, 'telling them, I know my place as I wish them to know theirs . . . to ask for my kinsman, Toby . . .'

'Belts and shackles!' this time Sir Toby exploded from the bush, and had to be hauled back by the combined strengths of Fabian and Sir Andrew . . .

Malvolio's fantasy continued. 'I frown the while,' the sky was withered by his frown, 'perchance wind up my watch or play with . . . some rich jewel; Toby approaches; curtsies there to me . . .' Malvolio's face took on an air of pained dignity. He held a hand out to the imaginary Toby. 'I extend my hand to him thus, quenching my familiar smile with an austere regard of control . . .'

'And does not Toby give you a blow on the lips then?' shrieked Toby, muzzled instantly by Fabian, who was determined to see out this escapade, for he too had fallen foul of Malvolio's pinch-faced disapproval and felt that a ripe punishment for such a man would be a good day's work.

But now Malvolio's prancing feet had neared the letter that lay in wait for him. It was Maria's letter, faking the handwriting of Olivia, and laid carefully on the path for him to find . . .

'By my life, this is my lady's writing!' exclaimed Malvolio on cue. He unfolded the paper, carefully, and paying little attention to the possibility that such a letter might be private to her ladyship, began to read. 'Jove knows I love: but who? Lips do not move; no man must know,' he read the tantalising words aloud. And then a thought struck him. Transfixed, he stood there, clasping the letter to his chest, his face suddenly aflame with knowledge. If these words should be for him!

The watchers tittered. Could the man truly be so easily caught? A riddle, a few clues (some of the letters of Malvolio's name, which his brain deciphered slowly), and Maria's trap was set: Malvolio was utterly convinced the letter was from Olivia, writing in secret, to him.

He read on. 'If this fall into your hands, revolve.' Malvolio spun on his heels. 'In my stars I am above you.' He looked up. And then he understood the clue and drew a deep breath of pure, glorious satisfaction. Of course! *Lady* Olivia was of noble birth, and so above him . . . He returned with rapt attention to the letter: 'but be not afraid of greatness,' it went on. 'Some are born great, some achieve greatness, and some have greatness thrust upon them . . . Remember who commended your yellow stockings, and wished to see you always cross-gartered . . . If you return my love, let it appear in your smiling; your smiles become you well; therefore in my presence smile, dear my sweet, I beg you . . .'

Malvolio stood in silence, gazing at the glorious letter. Then he clasped it to his bosom. Then he raised his eyes to heaven. 'I will smile!' he cried, 'I will do everything that you wish!' and in a paroxysm of delight he rushed away, to clad himself in the yellow stockings and cross-garters, and to prepare the smile that would eclipse all smiles, for Olivia . . .

Unable to control their mirth any longer, Sir Toby, Fabian and Sir Andrew promptly fell out of the bush, and rolled across the path, stopping only when Maria appeared, eager to know if her letter had achieved the desired effect.

'Why, you have put him in such a dream,' gasped Sir Toby Belch, 'that when the image of it leaves him he must run mad!'

'If you will then see the fruits of this sport,' Maria interrupted her fellow plotters' raucous laughter, 'mark his first approach before my lady: he will come to her in yellow stockings, and . . .' she snorted with laughter, 'it is a colour she loathes; and cross-gartered, a fashion she detests; and he will smile upon her, which will now be so unsuitable to her mood . . .!'

Viola's discomfort was growing by the minute. Once more forced to visit Olivia on behalf of Duke Orsino, she must endure not merely her master's rejection, but now an open wooing of herself! Olivia, by turns made shy or bold as the throbs of love filled her with courage or plunged her into abject shame, now declared her love for Orsino's page!

'Cesario, by the roses of the spring, by maidhood, honour, truth and everything, I love you so!' she cried. 'In spite of all your pride, neither wit nor reason can hide my passion.'

'By innocence I swear, and by my youth, I have one heart, one bosom and one truth, and that no woman has,' Viola cried. What was she to do in this extraordinary predicament? Such ardent sighs from Lady Olivia! Such gleaming eyes! Such longing hand-clasps, from which Viola escaped only with difficulty. 'Nor shall anyone be mistress of my heart except I alone,' she protested frantically. 'And so, farewell, good madam!'

This must, she promised herself, be absolutely the last visit to the countess for her master. She could endure this miserable confusion for not a minute more!

Sir Andrew Aguecheek was most unhappy. He had seen the countess pay more attention in a few moments to the duke's new page than she had paid in *weeks* to hopeful Andrew Aguecheek.

And with this he had finally seen enough. He would not stay a moment longer!

Sir Toby was made suddenly aware that the fat purse that lined their days with comforts was about to be whisked beyond his reach. Instantly, Sir Toby and Fabian were awash with words of hearty encouragement: the problem (as they put it to the disappointed knight) was that Olivia was watching to see how Sir Andrew would perform against this upstart page. The answer to the problem lay simply in challenging page Cesario to a duel. Would not such a duel be closely watched by Lady Olivia? Was she not plainly eager to know how her favoured suitor, good Sir Andrew, would fare!

So was the pouting Sir Andrew transformed again. He set off much cheered to write his challenge to the page who dared to try to claim Olivia's heart from him!

Sebastian and Antonio had at last arrived in town. Antonio, concerned not to be seen by any who would recognize him, had gone straight to find them lodgings in the suburbs and arranged to meet Sebastian there later. Sebastian set off to wander curiously around the town, to look at the sights for which the place was famed, and do a little shopping with the money which good Antonio had left him for his use, stowed safely in Antonio's own purse.

Meanwhile Olivia had sent for Cesario again. She waited nervously for the arrival of this youth, for she was by now so deeply in love with him that her whole existence seemed to hang on her adoration of him. She had forgotten what it was once like not to know him or to love him.

She waited, pacing before the door, wringing her hands, straightening her hair, her skirt . . . how exactly should she behave towards Cesario? What could she do to win his love?

For her pains, she got not Cesario, but Malvolio. And what a
Malvolio! Brilliant in sunshine-yellow stockings, like some gigantic
stalking bird, his legs laced most exotically with intricate cross-
gartering, a smile from ear to ear like an enormous wound from which
his teeth loomed, glistening . . . and such a wealth of knowing nods and
winks, and kissing hands towards Olivia . . .

Olivia drew back in horror, quite unprepared for this transformation
of her sober steward. Was this the man she relied on utterly to maintain
the calm and smooth-running of a sombre house of mourning? The
poor man must be dreadfully ill!

And there he was, leering and winking again, while all the while the
strangest of words dropped from his ever-smiling mouth . . .

'Be not afraid of greatness!' he grinned grotesquely at Olivia and

twirled a shapely yellow-gartered leg; 'it was well written,' he assured her. 'Some are born great, some achieve greatness . . .' he pranced before her, his smile stretching till it seemed to split his face in two. Then, with a string of wild flourishes with one flapping hand, he bent low before Olivia, to grimace ludicrously into her startled face, 'and some have greatness thrust upon them!' he finished, with a knowing wink.

Olivia, of course, knew nothing of the fake letter which had provided Malvolio's guide for this inspired performance. These antics from her usually impeccable steward were beyond her comprehension. There was no explanation for it but that the poor, blighted man had gone quite mad. With news of Cesario's arrival distracting her, she hastily gave orders that Malvolio should be taken care of, for she would not have harm come to him for all the world . . .

So it was that Sir Toby came to be entrusted with the care of 'mad' Malvolio! What a perfect place from which to exact revenge . . . and what a revenge it proved to be!

If Malvolio was behaving in a fashion for which the only explanation was his madness, why then mad he would be called, and with what gusto did Sir Toby, Sir Andrew, Fabian and Feste enter into this scheme of Malvolio's madness. Malvolio could not open his mouth, but that his audience squealed at the poor man's confusion of wit, he could not utter a single sound, but that they berated the 'foul fiends and devils' which had taken possession of his soul . . . And the more they baited Malvolio, the angrier, ruder, and more arrogant the man became, for had not the letter also said he should deal roughly with servants, rudely with kinsman . . .?

It all fitted so perfectly with Malvolio's expectations, and the letter had stroked his vanity with such audacity, that he followed, nose up in the air, right into the trap without a suspicion in the world that this was anything other than the device by which his mistress wished to show her secret love for him and urge him to show his love for her!

Sir Toby in revenge was ruthless. In a trice he had confined his victim in a pitch dark room, bound hand and foot for being a madman, there to endure his plight until such time as Toby might feel pity for the man . . .

Meanwhile Sir Toby's main concern was to keep Sir Andrew and his purse firmly in Olivia's house.

71

That hopeful knight had valiantly struggled off to write a challenge to 'Cesario'. He returned with some writing which was as addled as his meagre brain. This prize he entrusted proudly to Sir Toby, to be conveyed with all due ceremony to Cesario.

Behind his back, Sir Toby and Fabian were quick to hide what Sir Andrew had written. If Cesario should read this missive from the 'challenger', he could not help but see the towering heights of idiocy, not bravery, that spurred on the aged knight who dared him to a duel.

Instead, Sir Toby waylaid Cesario and most eloquently conveyed Sir Andrew's challenge by word of mouth. So vivid was the report of Sir Andrew Aguecheek's bravery and skill, his fury, deadly speed and daring, that it would have sent any youth into a state of nervousness about the safety of his life. It sent Cesario into a state of abject terror, for Viola had never even held a weapon in her hand and possessed neither the slightest skill, nor any will to fight. The prospect of duels, blood and death merely curdled her brain, transformed her strong straight legs into trembling pins that buckled at the knees, her arms into quivering rubber that had no strength even to hold the offending sword, and her voice, which she normally succeeded in pitching low enough to have some semblance of a young man's tones, to a pitiful squeak . . . the more so because the poor girl did not have the faintest idea what should have caused such anger against her.

All her efforts to escape the duel only caught her faster in the trap: according to Sir Toby Belch, a knight like fierce Sir Andrew Aguecheek would let no one rest until his challenge had been answered . . .

Returning as swiftly as his bloated bulk allowed, Sir Toby filled Sir Andrew's reeling head with terrors of a similar sort. This page of Duke Orsino's was a very devil! Such a skill with swords! There was no peace to be made with such a man: nothing but a duel to the death would satisfy him!

Sir Andrew swayed and would have fainted, but Sir Toby marched the wilting knight towards his doom . . .

His doom, in the shape of Viola praying that the ground would open up and swallow her, grew deathly pale. She beheld this bringer of destruction march towards her, and saw he was held back from his thirst for blood only by the sheer strength of his two companions! She trembled, and clutched at the sword Toby had thrust into her hands . . .

'Put up your sword!' the fierce cry seemed to come from nowhere, and like a thunderbolt from heaven, a man leapt out in front of her, his broad shape blocking off the waving sword of Andrew Aguecheek. 'If this young gentleman has done offence, I take the fault on me,' he shouted at the knight. 'If you offend *him*, I defy you for him!' and standing belligerently before Viola, the stranger held his own weapon menacingly, daring anyone to move towards her . . .

The speed with which her fate had been transformed from certain death to daring rescue by a total stranger was too much for Viola. Relief and shock flooded over her and turned her legs to water . . .

Who was this man? She had never seen him before, nor the soldiers who burst in and set upon her saviour, and had him bound between two stout guards before her brain had even recovered from the last shock. Arrested! By Duke Orsino's men!

And there was more. Now this stranger turned a look of love on her, and in a gruff, gentle voice, spoke as though he knew her!

'This comes with seeking you,' Antonio said, for Viola's rescuer was none other than this loyal friend of her own brother, Sebastian. And Antonio looked with sorrow on the youth that he had just rescued, whom he believed *was* Sebastian. 'But there's no remedy; I shall answer it. But my necessity makes me ask you for my purse . . .'

Purse? She had no purse of his! Viola began to wonder now if she was going mad.

Antonio halted, having seen her look of blank denial. He searched her face. A look of disbelieving horror crept across it. Denied! Thrown off when most he needed help! He tried again. 'I must ask you for some of that money.'

'What money, sir?' Viola asked in all innocence. 'For the fair kindness you have showed me here, I'll lend you something!'

He appealed in desperation to the soldiers who still held him fast. 'This youth that you see here I snatched one half out of the jaws of death . . . But oh how vile an idol is this god! Sebastian . . .!'

Sebastian! Viola's brain could barely hold the word. This man mistook her for another called Sebastian! A surge of thoughts rushed through her head: her own brother Sebastian looked very much like she did . . . even his clothes would be a little like the ones she wore, for it was Sebastian's style that she had followed in making up her page's clothes . . .

Could this stranger's Sebastian be her own brother? Could brother Sebastian be, after all these months, alive?

Sebastian, ignorant of the grim fate that had befallen his good friend Antonio, and still wandering idly about the town, filled up his time with small activities to erase the misery that filled his heart at memories of his sister's death.

Imagine then his irritation when he was accosted by a cheeky jester who claimed to know him well, and claimed he had been sent to find him by his mistress!

'Go to, you are a foolish fellow,' Sebastian retorted. 'Let me be rid of you.'

'No, I do not know you,' Feste mocked, for it was he. 'Nor am I sent to you by my lady to bid you come and speak with her; nor your name is not Master Cesario; nor this is not my nose, neither. Nothing that is so is so!'

'I beg you, vent your folly somewhere else. You do not know me,'

Sebastian dismissed him.

But hardly had he turned from this than he was set upon by a great beanpole of a gentleman who waved a sword as though it were a wand and stabbed the air with it, egged on by a monstrous, bloated wine-barrel of a man . . .

'Are all the people mad?' Sebastian yelled, drawing his sword to defend himself, and dealing the prancing knight a solid, no-nonsense blow.

Sir Andrew, who had been hit in the arm, and Sir Toby who had been hit nowhere but in his expectations that they were going to thrash their victim soundly, . . . stared in some confusion at the youth they thought was young Cesario. What, quaking at the knees a moment ago when the soldiers came, and now no less than a raging tiger of a man! Incensed, Sir Toby grabbed Sir Andrew's sword . . .

'Hold, Toby; on your life, I charge you, hold!' Olivia's furious voice rang out and stopped even Sir Toby in his bull-like rush towards his quarry.

'Ungracious wretch,' she hurled at him. 'Out of my sight!' Then she turned with such a glow of love towards Sebastian. 'Be not offended, dear Cesario,' she calmed him, and her tones were golden honey with the warmth of adoration in them.

Sebastian stood rooted to the ground in wonderment, disbelief and awe (tinged with an adventurer's lightning flash of insight at his miraculous good fortune). Apparently there was one Cesario much sought after in these parts, and much beloved by this jewel of a lady! Apparently he, Sebastian, was being mistaken for this Cesario. So either *they* were mad, or *he* was mad, or else this was a dream; and if it was a dream, why then, let him sleep on . . .

While all the world ran circles round Sebastian, believing him to be Cesario, and Antonio was arrested defending Cesario, believing him to be Sebastian, Malvolio was still shut away and treated as a madman by Sir Toby and his accomplices.

Now they persuaded Feste to dress up in a gown and beard and go to him: adopting a priest's solemn, sing-song tones, Feste duly hailed Malvolio through the tiny window of his dismal prison.

From inside there came the startled cry 'Who calls there?'

'Sir Topas the priest, who comes to visit Malvolio the lunatic,'

75

intoned Feste the jester.

'Sir Topas, Sir Topas, good Sir Topas, go to my lady,' pleaded Malvolio, the hood-winked steward. 'Never was a man thus wronged: good Sir Topas do not think me mad: they have laid me here in hideous darkness!' and at this last the poor man's voice quite broke with the horror and the terror of his plight.

Listening, even Sir Toby felt a twinge of some regret, though it was less for Malvolio's plight than for his own.

'Go to him in your own voice,' he urged Feste, 'bring me word how you find him. I wish we were well rid of this joke. If he could be conveniently released, I wish he were, for I am now so far out of favour with my niece that I cannot go any further with this sport . . .'

The familiar tones of Feste the jester reached Malvolio in his darkened cell and new hope surged through his black despair.

'Good fool,' he begged the jester with a respect he had never used before to him, 'Good fool, help me to a candle, pen, ink and paper: as I am a gentleman, I will live to be thankful to you for it.'

'Master Malvolio?' Feste enquired, with mock surprise.

'They keep me in darkness and do all they can to keep me out of my wits,' Malvolio cried. 'Good fool, help me to some light and some paper,' he repeated his pitiful refrain. 'I tell you, I am as well in my wits as any man in Illyria . . .'

On the question of how mad or sane were the people of Illyria, Sebastian at least would have been hard put to give a clear reply. Here was he, snatched from the jaws of death, plunged deep in sorrow for his sister's death, transported suddenly into a world of glory where the most exquisite lady (a countess, no less, and wealthy, too) adored him . . .

'This is the air; that is the glorious sun,' he told himself. 'This pearl she gave me, I do feel it and see it; and though it is wonder that surrounds me, yet it is not madness.' But then again, could he be certain of that?

And where was Antonio? His disappearance was bewildering. Sebastian had looked in vain for him at their arranged meeting place. Antonio had indeed been there, and had after scoured the town searching for Sebastian. But since, the man had disappeared!

And even as he pondered this strangest of strange accidents which brought him into the arms of this exquisite lady, Olivia herself appeared. She brought a priest with her, and now she begged Cesario (for so she believed Sebastian to be), to vow before the priest that he would marry her!

She stared breathlessly at Sebastian, in that instant suddenly appalled at her own audacity . . .

'What do you say?' she whispered, hardly daring to hear Cesario's answer. How little time had passed since she pursued Cesario with little encouragement to love, and yet how swiftly his cool rejection had become an ardent passion . . .

Now, waiting nervously for his reply, her fears were swiftly put to rest. 'Cesario' clasped her to his heart, and answered, 'I'll go with you; and having sworn truth, ever will be true.'

The Duke Orsino could stand no more rejection from Olivia. For months he had sung of his love by letter, messenger, gifts, poems, and nothing had won her heart. Now he came himself.

And Viola came too, nervous for her lord and for herself . . . she dared not think what might happen next!

What was to become of this appalling tangle of events? Orsino loved a woman, who loved Orsino's page, who was a woman hiding as a man, who loved Orsino . . .

They got no further than Olivia's garden.

'Here comes the man, sir, that rescued me!' Viola cried, relieved that she could show her saviour to the duke, for he alone could release Antonio from his guards.

The duke eyed the man slowly. 'That face I do remember well, yet when I saw it last, it was besmeared in the smoke of war . . .' he told Viola. 'He was the captain of a vessel that grappled with the most noble ship of our fleet . . .'

'He did me kindness, sir, drew his weapon in my defence, though in doing so he spoke so strangely . . .'

Antonio had been standing there, his dark eyes fixed in smouldering defiance on Viola. This final betrayal was too much for him. 'Orsino, noble sir,' he burst out, 'that most ungrateful boy there by your side . . .' in a fury of hurt he poured out his tale: how he had snatched the youth from raging seas, had brought him back to life and grown to love him . . . how he had thrown all care to the winds to follow him, protect him, care for him . . . for which he had received only betrayal, denial, and the crowning insult . . . 'he even denied me my own purse which I gave him for his use not half an hour before!'

'When did he come to this town?' Orsino asked, intrigued, for clearly the man spoke with an honest belief in the truth of his own tale.

'Today, my lord,' Antonio replied, 'and for three months before, both day and night, we did keep company.'

'Fellow, your words are madness,' the duke assured him, 'for three months this youth has waited upon me . . .' but even this engaging mystery was put to sudden flight from Orsino's mind, for Olivia had entered the room, and Orsino had no eyes for anyone else.

Olivia, however, had no eyes for any but Cesario.

Though she was courteous enough in greeting to the duke, her gaze was fastened only on his page.

'Cesario, you do not keep promise with me,' she challenged, with a look of hurt.

The duke heard this at first with incomprehension. But having once again tried to gain Olivia's attention and found it was locked fast on young Cesario, a new thought entered the rejected lover's brain. It was Cesario the lady loved!

This final rejection was more than he could stand; he could be as cruel as she! He would take away this youth that she adored, to spite her love . . .

Now Olivia saw her passionate lover of a few hours ago, willingly prepared to go off with the duke!

'Where does Cesario go?' she cried.

'After him I love more than I love these eyes, more than my life, more than ever I shall love wife,' Viola declared, throwing all caution off, and turning ardently towards her lord.

Orsino looked at her in some surprise. This passion, though he knew the youth was fond of him, was not expected. Viola, feeling her loved one's searching eyes on her, raised hers and met his gaze, then in confusion flushed deep red . . .

'Cesario, husband, stay,' shrieked Olivia.

'Husband!' yelled the duke. Betrayed by his page!

This appalling truth was instantly confirmed by the priest who had married them not two hours before!

Viola heard this information with horror no less than that which filled the duke. She stared from Olivia to Orsino, whose look of rage and hurt almost wilted her. That he should think she would betray him thus; that Olivia could believe she would betray him thus . . .!

Olivia, for her part, looked from Orsino to Viola in panic. Where was the eager lover of two hours ago, the man who had leapt to her love with the heat of passion that matched her own?

While all the while Antonio looked on, scowling at Viola, as did Orsino, as did Olivia, each believing this youth to be a master of betrayal, a man without a soul, heart or honour of any kind . . .

Into this bewildered circle stumbled Sir Andrew with bleeding head, followed by Toby Belch, clutching his head and moaning, fleeing (so they said) from the duke's young gentleman, Cesario, who had viciously set upon them but a moment ago . . .

And there he stood! Even Sir Toby now shrank a little from the sight of him . . .

Everyone stared at Viola. A liar, a betrayer, and now a breaker of men's heads!

And a man who could by magic split himself in two! For suddenly a second Cesario sprang before their astounded eyes. 'I am sorry, madam, I have hurt your kinsman,' he cried out to Lady Olivia. 'Pardon me, sweet one, even for the vows we made each other, so little time ago!'

There was a silence. Olivia stared from the Cesario who acknowledged his vows to her to the Cesario who denied them. Viola gazed with fast-beating heart upon this mirror-image of herself and scarcely dared to hope . . .

The duke whispered, 'One face, one voice and two persons!' While Sebastian, for the new-comer was he, spotted Antonio and rushed towards him with his hands outstretched, 'Antonio, oh my dear Antonio! How have the hours racked and tortured me, since I have lost you!'

'Sebastian, are you he?' said Antonio, suspiciously, for the misery of these past hours had wiped away his trust of any man. 'How have you made division of yourself? An apple, sliced in two, is not more twin than these two creatures! Which is Sebastian?'

For the first time, Sebastian became aware of his other self. He gaped at the apparition: what new madness in this land of madness was this trick? He laughed, for perhaps the trick would laugh itself away. But

still it stood there, and still the duke, Olivia, and Antonio stood looking at them both, from one to the other and back again.

'I never had a brother. Nor can I be here and everywhere!' Sebastian assured them, though by now he was beginning to wonder if he could say even this with any certainty. 'But I had a sister . . .' and even as he said this, a new hope began to stir in him . . .

Viola took a step towards him. 'Sebastian was my father; such a Sebastian was my brother, too . . .' for in that moment she, at least, had understood . . .

'Were you a woman,' cried Sebastian, 'I would let my tears fall upon your cheek, and say, "welcome, drowned Viola!"'

With a sweep Viola tore the cap from off her head and let her long hair tumble down. 'My father had a mole upon his brow!' she cried.

' And so had mine,' yelled Sebastian.

' And died that day that Viola turned thirteen!' Viola shrieked, and fell upon her brother's neck in tears of joy.

And so the tangle was untied, and all explained, forgiven, and repaired. Olivia, who had unwittingly loved a girl and believed herself betrayed, now found herself united, as she longed for, with a man. Viola, whose sorrow for her brother's death had remained with her for

three long months, was now miraculously clasped in his living arms.
And the duke . . .

The duke had watched these moments of revelation and discovery
with fascination. As the truth began to dawn on him, so was his heart
and mind awash with sudden memories of all the months in which his
devoted page had offered him companionship, and sympathy . . . and
love . . .

He turned now to gaze at Viola with an eye and heart uncluttered by his worship of Olivia. He looked at Viola not as a gentle youth to whom he gave his confidence, but as a woman, and in that instant, knew he loved her as he had never loved Olivia. He loved her as a person that he knew and understood and truly cared for, not an idol that he painted in his mind in colours that were not her own . . .

And he remembered her own words to him. 'Boy,' he said, with a teasing mockery in his eyes, 'you have said to me a thousand times that you never would love any woman as you loved me . . .'

'And all those sayings will I swear again,' Viola said, throwing all caution to the winds, 'and all those swearings keep as true in soul as is the sun that keeps the day from night . . .'

'Give me your hand, and let me see you in your woman's clothes,' Orsino cried.

And so two pairs of tangled lovers were untangled, and retied with the one they loved: Sebastian to Olivia and Orsino to Viola.

But two others languished still alone: Antonio knew that he had lost the companionship of the young man he adored; but yet there was a compensation in the knowledge that no betrayal of his trust had taken place.

And Malvolio? What of Malvolio, poor hood-winked Malvolio, whose fantasy of love had led him to a trap beyond his wildest nightmares?

Followed closely by Malvolio, Feste the jester, true to his word, now delivered a letter from that poor despairing man to Olivia . . .

And so it came about that Maria's letter, faking Olivia's handwriting was produced. In a moment the plot was laid before Olivia, Malvolio's plight revealed in all its misery, as was the role of Toby, Fabian and Maria and the jester, to say nothing of Sir Andrew Aguecheek . . . Though these admissions were not given without a full and vivid catalogue of those injuries at Malvolio's hand that had prompted them all to take revenge . . .

'Alas, how they have baffled you,' sighed Olivia to Malvolio.

'And thus the whirligig of time brings in his revenges,' Feste chanted.

'I'll be revenged on the whole pack of you,' declared Malvolio, his nose returning to its customary height above the ground, his mouth to its customary pinched pout, whirling on his heel with his customary

82

snort, to march away from them.

'He has been notoriously abused,' said Olivia, watching the offended man disappear from sight with sorrow.

'Pursue him,' urged Orsino, for whom no cloud would mar this day of unexpected happiness. 'Entreat him to a peace.' And now he turned with joy towards his faithful page.

'Cesario, come, for so you shall be, while you are a man; but when in other garments you are seen, Orsino's mistress, and his fancy's queen!'

And now the garden of this stately home in fair Illyria was emptied of its lovers gained and lovers lost. Only the jester Feste stayed, to linger in the fading sunshine, and to sing a little, mournful song . . .

'When that I was and a little tiny boy,
With a hey, ho, the wind and the rain,
A foolish thing was but a toy,
For the rain it raineth every day . . .'

The Taming of The Shrew

It was a tinker's vision, or a tinker's dream, this story of the taming of
the shrew. Or was it the vision of a lord who only thought he was a
tinker? The tinker couldn't tell, and still can't from that day, long ago,
to this . . .

At any rate, it happened to one Christopher Sly, by birth a pedlar, by
education a card-maker turned bear-herd, by profession a tinker. By
day he roamed the countryside of Warwickshire rattling pots and
kettles. By night he drowned himself in ale, and fell more often than not
into a drunken stupor in the courtyard of the ale-house on the heath.

This ale-house was in good hunting country, and so it was that a rich
lord came by, with all his hunting men and dogs. The lord was in high
spirits and good humour. The day's hunting had gone well, and there
was nothing in the world he enjoyed more than this business of the
chase, with horns and dogs and horses galloping . . .

In this merry mood, he spied the drunken bundle. He poked it, and
discovered the tinker snorting more like grunting pig than snoring
human. Straightaway the lord had the grand idea of playing a trick on
him. What merry sport there'd be if he could spirit off this drunkard,
install him in the grand chamber of his country mansion, clean, polish
and perfume him, wrap him in rich garments, play soft music and when
he woke have all the servants bow and scrape as though he were a
mighty lord emerging from a long period of madness in which he only
thought he was a poor tinker by the name of Sly!

And then, to further befuddle the bewildered man, the lord's young
page could deck himself in women's clothes and present himself as the
simpering, dimpled lady of the house, Sly's pretty wife! To crown it all
there'd be an enchanting spectacle to delight the eye and tickle the
tinker's fancy, to transport him off into the realms of exquisite fantasy:

he would watch a play performed by strolling players.

So it came about that tinker-turned-lord and page-turned-lady sat in the gallery of the great hall of a stately country mansion, Sly no longer knowing if he slept or woke, was tinker or a lord, trapped in a tinker's or a lord's strange fantasy . . .

Though what with the pretty lady by his side (he leered at her, and slid a little closer, she simpered and slid away) and what with silks and perfumes, and wine and food, he no longer cared to know. And so he blinked his blearing eyes, and craned his neck, and down below him in the stately hall began the players' tale . . .

It was the jovial comedy of Katharine, known to all of Padua as the shrew . . . and thus, before the tinker's dazzled eyes, miraculously, the stately hall in Warwickshire began to fade, and as the tale unfolded, this tinker, who had never strayed beyond the boundaries of Warwickshire, beheld instead the sun-lit streets and brilliant skies of ancient Padua in Italy, and heard the bell-filled towers ringing, ringing in his ears . . .

In Padua, stuffed in equal measure with its men of learning in the ancient university and with its merchants rattling money-bags in the exchange, Katharine was famous. But it was not for learning, nor for riches. It was her tongue that spread her fame near and far. Never was a tongue so sharply wagged as Katherine's! Never was a lady so disgruntled and ill-tempered!

She was handsome, and she was rich, and she was young: all perfect virtues for a lady ripe for marriage. But there was no man in all of Padua would take her, at any price: they feared either to be sizzled by the woman's scalding tongue, or have her practise on their heads with three-legged stools for weapons: tongue and furniture she wielded with equal skill. There were, on the other hand, several men in Padua who would pay their fortunes to have her younger sister Bianca for a wife. *She* was a girl framed in heaven, angelic, gentle, modest, well-behaved and decorous, as should all wives of Padua be.

Two suitors in particular, were running neck and neck across the field: one young, by name of Hortensio, one old, by name of Gremio, but neither, it seemed, to be satisfied. Katharine's father, unable to endure the nightmare of Katharine on his hands for ever more, had decreed that there could be no husband for Bianca, till there was a husband found for sister Katharine. Meanwhile, declared the adamant father, angelic Bianca would undertake her studies: she took most delight (as did all angels) in poetry and music. A schoolmaster was needed, not a husband! And he would brook no argument.

The would-be suitors listened to the father's words with horror. A husband found for Katharine! Doomsday would come before a man would take this witch! Gloomily they viewed their prospects: neither could advance till Katharine was safely stowed in marriage. Their rivalry for Bianca's hand must, without question, take second place to the urgent task of netting a husband for the cursing shrew.

But fortune was on their side. It appeared in the unlikely shape of a young man of Verona named Petruchio. Now this Petruchio was, if nothing else, a scrupulously honest man, and to his friends he confessed with not the slightest hesitation that he had come to Padua to find a wife. This wife must above all be wealthy (Petruchio's father having died recently and left him a lot of land, but little money). So the young man came, to seek his fortune and to wive and thrive in Padua.

He confided to Hortensio that if Hortensio knew a woman rich enough to be Petruchio's wife, whether she was rough as the swelling Adriatic seas, whether she was foul, old or cursed, he'd take her. 'I come to wive it wealthily in Padua: if wealthily, then happily in Padua!'

Dare Hortensio suggest Katharine? Tentatively he did, but confessed *he* would not wed her for a mine of gold.

'Hortensio, peace!' Petruchio said. 'You do not know the effects of gold!' Having set his mind briskly to this bold project, he was as eager as any suitor to see the blushing bride (and enquire more on the question of the height and breadth of her marriage dowry).

In return for a rapid introduction to old Baptista, the lady's father, Hortensio asked a single favour of Petruchio. Since her father's stern decree, he was denied all access to his adored Bianca. But if Petruchio would present him (heavily disguised) as a sober music-master he could stay close to his jewel and pip old Gremio to the winning post!

Meanwhile old Gremio was also busy advancing his suit to Bianca. Or so he thought. Most fortuitously, he too had found a schoolmaster. He hurried to present him to Signior Baptista.

Unfortunately for Gremio this schoolmaster was no schoolmaster, just as Hortensio was no music-master, Sly was no Lord and his lady was no lady! This schoolmaster was none other than a third suitor for angelic Bianca's hand. Lucentio of Florence by name, and a handsome young man of considerable wealth, he had been sent to Padua to pursue his studies at the university and do some business for his father.

No sooner had he and his lively servant Tranio arrived in that bustling city, than he had caught a glimpse of sweet Bianca. From that moment his eyes could take in nothing else.

'Tranio, I burn,' he wailed. 'I pine, I perish, Tranio! Counsel me, Tranio, for I know you can. Assist me, Tranio, for I know you will.'

Tranio was never short of ideas, and in a moment their scheme was plotted. Lucentio would transform himself into a schoolmaster and use the ancient money-bags, old Gremio, to present himself to Baptista. Meanwhile Tranio would adopt his master's role, and decked out in a gentleman's finery, present himself to Padua as Lucentio. He would keep house for him, entertain his father's friends, and do all those little tasks of business for which they had been sent here . . . (and Tranio rubbed his hands in relish at the thought).

And so with gentlemen transformed to schoolmasters, servant transformed to gentleman, and fortune hunter transformed to loving suitor, they gathered at Baptista's house, to woo fair, gentle, modest Bianca, and her fiery-tempered sister, Katharine.

'Hortensio, have you told him *all* her faults,' gasped Gremio, staring at Petruchio in open admiration. He was transfixed by the sight of any man who would willingly take on a vixen. 'Will you woo this wild-cat?' he wanted to know, to be absolutely sure.

'Do you think a little din can daunt my ears?' scorned brave Petruchio. 'Have I not in my time heard lions roar? And do you tell me of a woman's tongue that does not give half so great a blow to hear as will a chestnut in a farmer's fire?'

Thus reassured, the rivals Hortensio and Gremio (turned allies till such time as Katharine was wed), agreed to stand the cost of Petruchio's wooing. And thus inspired, Petruchio sealed the deal.

But now, to complicate the matter, a most elegant young gentleman, glorious in the very latest fashions, pranced along the street towards them. To the consternation of all but Lucentio (who recognized his trusty servant Tranio, dressed up splendidly as Lucentio) this dainty apparition announced that he too was a suitor for Bianca's hand. But he redeemed himself in the eyes of all concerned by adding the weight of his fat purse to the coffers designed to spur Petruchio to woo and wed the scolding daughter and release the other from her miserable suitorless imprisonment in Baptista's house.

Inside the house, it was like hell on earth: doors slammed, furniture crashed, Bianca wept, Katharine shouted, and Baptista raged. Katharine was incensed by her sister's 'gentleness' and 'modesty', by her ready fund of suitors, and by her father's doting gaze upon the simpering beauty. Attempts to taunt her sister to confess which of her suitors she really loved had failed, for the simple reason that Bianca, to be honest, loved none of them. Katharine had tied her hands and hauled her round the room, slapped her for her silence, and was glaring now at her furious father, come to rescue his frail treasure.

'Her silence flouts me, and I'll be revenged,' yelled Katharine, and flew at her sister with clenched fists.

Baptista rescued his younger daughter and stared at the older one in black despair. Was ever a gentleman plagued with such a daughter? He was somewhat preoccupied with this thought and more than a little weary to be faced again with a flock of hopeful suitors for Bianca. So he paid little attention to the arrival of some six or seven gentleman, among whom he detected the ever eager grey-haired Gremio.

Imagine then his disbelief, excitement and delight on being asked about a fair virtuous daughter named Katharine!

'I have a daughter, sir, called Katharine,' he confirmed, for, being an honest man, he did not trust himself to say much more.

'I am a gentleman of Verona, sir,' the enquirer said, 'that hearing of her beauty and her wit, her affability and her bashful modesty, her wondrous qualities and her mild behaviour, am bold to show myself a forward guest within your house, to make my eye a witness of that report . . .' So saying, without a single blush at such a pack of lies, Petruchio presented Hortensio as a music-master, skilled also in mathematics. Unrecognizable behind an enormous wig and even more enormous spectacles, Hortensio struggled with the voluminous folds of a scholar's sober gown in black, and peered owlishly at them.

Baptista received the music-master graciously, but returned his attention quickly to the more fascinating subject of Petruchio. Was this man *serious* in his desire to see Katharine? Could there *truly* be a possible end to this devilish nightmare? But before he could discover any more, old Gremio, not to be outdone, pushed forward *his* schoolmaster (disguised Lucentio), skilled in Greek, Latin and other languages, as any respectable schoolmaster should be . . . Whereupon Tranio, pretending to be Lucentio, announced himself as a further suitor for the angel's hand, and presented a parcel of books and a lute to be used in their instruction.

Baptista stood amazed. Three suitors for one daughter (and this latter, the son of a wealthy, well-known merchant of Verona), *two* schoolmasters, and the tools of their trade, and now, the crowning glory, a suitor for Katharine? Quickly he despatched the schoolmasters to the daughters so that he could get on with the vital task of finding out how serious was this man Petruchio in his designs upon his daughter.

Most serious it seemed. The negotiation proved profitable on both sides. Petruchio presented his credentials with a flourish: son of Antonio, who had left him all his lands and goods. And, swiftly to the point, 'If I get your daughter's love, what dowry shall I have with her?' Petruchio enquired.

Baptista, already settled on this most presentable of sons-in-laws, offered a small fortune to sweeten the bitter pill of Katharine: one half of all his lands after his death, and straightaway, twenty thousand crowns in money. All that remained was to capture the shrew's love. Baptista's eager face clouded with gloom as he came down to earth again. But Petruchio, the bargain so successfully concluded, was undaunted.

'Why, that is nothing; for I tell you, father, I am as haughty as she proud-minded; and where two raging fires meet together they do consume the thing that feeds their fury. Though little fire grows great with little wind, yet extreme gusts will blow out fire and all; for I am rough and woo not like a babe . . .'

And it was a good thing that his mind was so made up, for any other might have on that instant fled, to behold poor Hortensio, his wig awry, his spectacles smashed, and his head popped through the belly of the lute like a startled chick from a shattered egg. Katharine did not like Hortensio's criticism of her playing. She had used the earnest tutor for an anvil, and hammered the lute straight down on his head!

'It is a lusty wench,' declared Petruchio. 'I love her ten times more than ever I did: Oh, how I long to have some chat with her!'

Now he'd got the measure of the shrewish girl, his plot was fully formed and he was ready for the wooing. If she yelled, he would tell her that she sang as sweetly as a nightingale; if she frowned, he'd tell her that she looked as clear as morning roses newly washed with dew; and if she slumped in sullen silence, he would compliment her on her eloquence and charm. And, if she told him to be off, he'd thank her as though she'd begged him to stay a week . . .

She arrived, urged in by her excited father. She did not like the look of her first and only suitor. The first thing that Petruchio noticed was that she *was* beautiful, but that the beauty of her eye was dark with sullen fury and the curve of what should be a merry mouth was hung down with a sour pout.

'Good morrow, Kate; for that's your name, I hear,' cheerily he greeted her.

'Well you have heard, but something hard of hearing: they call me Katharine that do talk of me,' she answered rudely.

'You lie,' was Petruchio's spirited rejoinder. 'You are called plain Kate, and bonny Kate and sometimes Kate the cursed; but Kate, the prettiest Kate in Christendom, Kate of Kate Hall, my super-dainty Kate, and therefore Kate, hearing your mildness praised in every town, and your beauty sounded, I am moved to woo you for my wife.'

'Moved!' shrieked Katharine, 'let him that moved you here, *remove* you away again.'

'Come, come, you wasp,' said Petruchio, coaxing, 'in faith, you are too angry.'

'If I be waspish, best beware my sting,' snarled she.

'My remedy is then, to pluck it out,' retorted he.

'Aye, if the fool could find it where it lies!'

And so the wooing went in fine style. It ended, as did all conversations with hot-tempered Katharine, with a blow to Petruchio's head. 'I swear I'll cuff you, if you strike again,' he warned, catching her arm, and holding it, tightly. 'Come, Kate, come; you must not look so sour.'

'It is my fashion, when I see a crab!' she yelled.

'Why, here's no crab, and therefore look not sour,' replied Petruchio, still holding on.

'There is, there is,' she yelled again, struggling to free her arm.

'Then show it me.'

'Had I a glass, I would,' she sneered.

'What, you mean my face?' Petruchio asked, and pulled her closer to that part of him.

'You are withered,' Katharine said, trying not to look.

'It is with cares,' retorted he.

'I care not,' retorted she.

Petruchio let her go. He smiled at her, as though he smiled at the sweetest words that ever a girl had said to him. 'It was told me you were rough and coy and sullen,' he said, shaking his head, as though in disbelief. 'And now I find report a very liar: for you are pleasant, gamesome, courteous, sweet as spring-time flowers . . .'

Katharine glowered at him suspiciously.

He continued, unabashed, 'You cannot frown, nor bite your lip, as angry women do! Nor do you take your pleasure in cross talk, but entertain your wooers with such mildness!'

The glowering turned to fury, like a storm, in Katharine's eyes.

'Why does the world report that Kate does limp?' wondered Petruchio, out loud. 'Oh slanderous world! Kate like the hazel-twig is straight and slender and as brown in hue as hazel-nuts and sweeter than the kernels!'

'Go, fool,' she snorted, and turned on her heel.

'Therefore,' cried Petruchio, reaching her with a single bound and swinging her face to face with him, 'setting all this chat aside, thus, in plain terms – your father has consented that you shall be my wife. Your dowry is agreed on; and will you, nill you, I *will* marry you. You must be married to no man but me; for I am he that is born to tame you and bring you from a wild Kate to a Kate like other household Kates!'

And with this bold pronouncement he turned to greet the returning Baptista with assurances that Kate was modest as the dove, and mild as the morn, a statement which her father had some difficulty believing as his eldest daughter stood there in familiar style, cursing roundly at the 'mad-cap ruffian, one-half lunatic' as she called him, that her father had seen fit to set on her.

But it appeared that Petruchio had made up his mind, and on Sunday next he would marry her.

'I'll see you hanged on Sunday first,' muttered Kate.

'Oh, how much she loves me,' Petruchio cried, 'Oh the kindest Kate!' And with this Petruchio bounded off to Venice, as he said, to buy some clothes in honour of the wedding day.

So what was left, but to provide the feast and invite the guests?
Katharine was settled, despite her scowling rumblings, for when all was
said and done, her father's word was law.

And so Bianca was open to the field again. The suitors flooded in, like
flocks of cooing birds. Gremio claimed priority, for he had got there
first. Tranio, pretending to be Lucentio, claimed the greater love.
Baptista, ever the businessman at heart, declared the choice would rest
upon the store of wealth that each could offer as a husband.

The grey-beard money-bags, old Gremio, was well-prepared. He
conjured up his houses, silver, gold, rich furnishings, tapestries, linen,
coffers stuffed with money, to say nothing of his farm and plump dairy
livestock, all of which he pledged to fair Bianca.

Tranio, with the free generosity of one who can give away another's
wealth, announced he was his father's only heir, and produced two or
three houses more, and a chunk more land.

Gremio paled, but not to be outbid in the market-place, threw in his
land and a rich merchant ship at Marseilles.

Tranio, with the determination of one who would sacrifice all for his
master's passionate love, produced three merchant vessels, three large
sailing galleys and several smaller ones.

Gremio, sunk by this fleet, retired white-faced from the fray. Baptista
clapped the victorious Tranio on the back and declared that he could
marry Bianca on the Sunday following Katharine's wedding to
Petruchio.

Bianca had never realised what a world of fascination lay in learning
Latin. With her head bent close to her earnest young Latin master (the
music-master scowled suspiciously at this) Bianca had learned such
wonderful things as that *'Hic ibat'* meant 'I am Lucentio, son of
Vicentio of Pisa, *'Sigeia tellus'* could be marvellously translated as
'disguised thus to get your love,' and that snuggled down between the
words *'Hic steterat'*, *'Priami'* and *'celsa senis'* was the information that
the Lucentio that came wooing was but his servant Tranio, all set to
befuddle her father into consent to the true Lucentio marrying her, and
pip the greybeard Gremio, to say nothing of the distinctly amorous
music master, to the winning post.

93

Learning quickly how this Latin translation worked, Bianca rapidly proved her skill as a pupil and succeeded in translating '*Hic ibat Simois*' as 'I know you not,' '*hic est Sigeia tellus*' as 'I trust you not', '*Hic steterat Priami*' as 'take heed he hear us not,' and '*celsa senis*' as 'despair not', after which she graced her Latin master with a brilliant smile.

'Madam, it is in tune,' yelled Hortensio, who had been frantically tuning his new lute, as yet unbroken by Katharine, against Bianca's promise that when it was in tune she would indulge in a music lesson.

Bianca smiled again at the Latin master, and turned her attention to the learning of the instrument. And what a marvel this appeared: between the notes of the music scale, what should be lurking but

'I am the ground of all accord, to plead Hortensio's passion,
Bianca take him for your lord, that loves with all affection,
one clef, two notes have I, show pity, or I die!'

Unfortunately for the music master, Bianca had decided she did not enjoy this learning of the scales half so much as she liked Latin. Hortensio scowled even more suspiciously at the Latin master.

The day of Katharine's marriage dawned. There was, however, no sign of any bridegroom. Katharine had been pushed willy nilly into a wedding dress by her determined father and by a sister grown even more resolute since she had learned the infinite wonders of Latin grammar. No one paid the slightest attention to Katharine's scowls, yells, or warnings that Petruchio was raving mad. And now, to her mortification and eternal shame, the bridegroom had ignored the wedding: she, a girl without a suitor, was now a bride without a partner, and fair set to be the laughing-stock of Padua. In a fashion quite uncharacteristic of that strong-willed lady, she broke down weeping, and was led away by a sympathetic sister Bianca, though not without an exquisite hidden smile from that angelic lady towards the Latin master.

But Petruchio did come, eventually. And in what style! All Padua stood in admiration: a man set to wed the shrew of Padua, and in wedding clothes such as Padua had never seen: an old patched jacket and breeches, odd boots, one laced, the other buckled. And he rode a horse that had probably seen better days stuffed in a museum, to say nothing of the bridle and saddle which seemed to have been sorted from the dustbin, as had the bridegroom's broken sword.

'I am glad he comes, however he comes,' sighed old Baptista, for the moment much relieved. The thought of further days with Katharine in the house was almost too much to be endured.

Petruchio brushed any comment on his eccentric wedding clothes aside. 'To me she's married, not to my clothes,' he said.

The wedding was extraordinary. All the guests agreed on this, comparing notes thereafter. When the priest asked Petruchio if Katharine would be his wife, he swore so loud that the priest dropped his book, and as he stooped to pick it up, the mad-brained bridegroom dealt him such a blow that priest and book fell down again. The ceremony done, the bridegroom called for wine, gulped some and

emptied the rest over the sexton. Then he took the bride around the neck (Gremio paled with horror at the memory of it), and kissed her lips with such a smack that the whole church echoed with the clamour.

The wedding feast, prepared with joy by Baptista to celebrate a marriage he once thought would never happen, never did. Petruchio refused to stay, and when Katharine declared in characteristic tones that she refused to go, Petruchio seized her round the waist, hoisted her up for all the world as though she were a bundle of household goods, and defied anyone to stop him. 'I will be master of what is my own,' he yelled, waving his battered sword as though he planned to use it. 'She is my goods, my chattels; she is my house, my household stuff, my field, my barn, my horse, my ox, my ass . . . draw your weapon,' he shouted to his servant, 'we are beset with thieves. Rescue your mistress, if you be a man. Fear not, sweet wench,' he addressed the kicking bundle in his arms, 'they will not touch you, Kate,' and on this exotic note, bride, bridegroom and servant had disappeared.

'Let them go, a couple of quiet ones,' sighed Baptista, wearily.

'Of all the mad matches, there never was the like,' nodded Tranio.

And Bianca agreed that, being mad herself, Katharine was surely madly mated.

Katharine and Petruchio had reached Petruchio's country house. It had not been an easy journey. It was long, dark, muddy and cold, punctuated throughout by swearing and shouting from Petruchio, stumbling of horses and cuffing of servants. Katharine had fallen in the mud, for which Petruchio blamed his servant, and Katharine had even waded through the filth to rescue that poor man from being beaten soundly by his furious master.

The arrival at the house went off with similar gusto. Petruchio yelled, swore, swiped at the servants, found fault with everything, and was generally in very high spirits. Katharine was now exhausted, cold, bewildered, and (though she would never have admitted it) decidedly afraid that she was married to a genuine madman. She was almost faint with hunger.

But there was to be no eating, for Petruchio did not like the meat: it was burnt, he declared, and promptly threw it at the serving man. Burnt meat, he announced solemnly to Katharine, made one bad-tempered and should not be consumed. And with this remarkable observation, he carried his half-dead wife off to the bridal chamber.

The wedding night continued in fine style. Petruchio spent half the night flinging the pillows one way, the sheets another, and the blankets a third, complaining that the bed was badly made. The other half he spent declaiming, for the benefit of Kate, on all the subjects in the world on which he had any kind of opinion. Katharine no longer knew which way to stand, look or speak so as not to provoke him further, so much she longed for peace. She drifted as though in a dream, or more likely a madman's nightmare.

And so Petruchio began the taming of his Kate, by outkating Kate. Transformed into a scolding, cursing, ranting, railing madman of a husband, he hoped his exhausted, starved and frightened wife would stop, and look, and understand she faced the mirror image of herself.

Hortensio had found that nothing could persuade Bianca to embrace her music lessons with the same enthusiasm with which she undertook to learn Latin. He had also observed how this young Latin teacher produced the most ardent sighs, secret looks, and even quickly stolen kisses, when Bianca thought she was not being observed!

Disgusted, he decided that he would not deign to run in a field with so many competitors, and resolved to switch his affections forthwith to a wealthy widow who had sighed for him as long as he had sighed for ungrateful Bianca. But first, he'd go and see his friend Petruchio: if he was to indulge in marriage with a lusty widow, a few lessons on how Petruchio was taming the fearsome Katharine, might come in handy!

Katharine was almost in despair: starved, giddy for lack of sleep, for she lived on a diet of nothing but Petruchio's brawling humour, she was reduced to pleading bitterly for food from her husband's servants. They, well tuned for the drama by their implacable master, tantalized her with suggestions: a fat tripe? some beef and mustard? the beef without the mustard? or better still, the mustard without the beef? She flew at the servant with upraised fists, but it was all to no avail.

To show his love, Petruchio produced meat prepared by his own hands. Katharine stared greedily at it, and prepared to eat it ravenously without a word.

'I am sure, sweet Kate, this kindness merits thanks,' her torturing husband said. She stared hungrily from meat to him, as though she knew not which to eat first.

'What, not a word?' and before her stricken eyes the plate was spirited away again.

She leapt to her feet, 'I pray you, let it stand!'

'The poorest service is repaid with thanks; and so shall mine, before you touch the meat,' he said.

She glared at him. He glared at her. She looked down. Petruchio did not. She looked at the meat again, and her hunger screamed for mercy.

'I thank you, sir,' she said. The meat reappeared, and she ate it frantically before it disappeared again.

With some food inside her aching stomach, her spirits climbed a little higher. And then, as though the sunshine might return, suddenly Petruchio was all generosity. They would return at once to her father's house, he declared, decked out in rich new finery: coats and caps and rings and ruffs and cuffs and scarfs and fans . . . there was a tailor here already . . .

But as with food and bed-making, so with the clothes: no sooner had she cast her eyes on cap or gown she liked than it was whisked beyond her reach, not being to the taste of Petruchio.

'Gentlewomen wear such caps as these,' cried Katharine, who was still wearing the garments from her wedding day and craved a change almost as much as she craved sleep or food.

'When you are gentle, you shall have one too, and not till then,' her husband said. And with an oath or two towards the tailor, the clothes were gone.

But Petruchio insisted that they go at once to her father's house, poorly clad or otherwise.

'Go call my men, and let us go straight to him,' he cried. 'Let's see; I think it is now some seven o'clock, and well we may come there by midday.'

'I dare assure you sir, it is almost two; and it will be supper-time before you come there,' Katharine declared.

And for her pains received a withering glare. 'It shall be what o'clock I say it is,' her tyrannous husband yelled.

And Hortensio, who had by now arrived and observed the business of the meat, and then the business of the clothes, and finally the business of the clocks, shook his head in wonderment. 'Why, so this gallant will command the sun!' he observed.

It seemed that Petruchio heard him. They journeyed forward on the road to Padua, through a searing afternoon.

'Good Lord,' exclaimed Petruchio, 'how bright and goodly shines the moon!'

'The moon!' exclaimed Katharine, weary almost to death with all this madness. 'The sun! It is not moonlight now!'

'I say it is the moon that shines so bright,' Petruchio said.

'I know it is the sun that shines so bright,' said Katharine.

'It shall be moon, or star, or what I say,' said Petruchio, 'before I journey to your father's house. Go on, and fetch our horses back again!'

And mad-brained husband stared belligerently at fearsome Kate, who stared as obstinately back at him.

'Say as he says, or we shall never go,' begged Hortensio.

Katharine sighed. She was hot, tired, dusty, still hungry, and very thirsty. Ahead lay a seemingly endless journey, and it was not only the journey to her father's house that she was thinking of. This rocky path forward with this man Petruchio stretched endlessly ahead of her. At first the haphazard nature of his tempers had fired her fury and resentment. Then bewilderment and fear set in. And then a new, duller anger, that had plunged deep down. Now, as she sat quietly upon her horse, and listened to his ravings on the sun and moon, she saw something that she had not seen before. Listening to Petruchio was like listening to herself, once, in those far-off days before Petruchio.

And, she reflected, it was not a pleasant sound. She was writhing now beneath an ill-tempered, selfish, and stinging tongue, much as she had made others writhe . . . This idiocy of his made just as little, or just as much sense as her own had made, depending on which way up you looked at it.

She raised her gaze towards Petruchio, and it was suddenly with new eyes. And though she was not certain, she began, almost, to understand . . .

'Forward, I pray, since we have come so far,' she said, and she was talking about more than the road to Padua which lay before them. 'And be it moon, or sun, or what you please, even if you please to call it a candle, from now on it shall be so for me.'

'I say it is the moon,' said Petruchio, exulting inwardly.

'I know it is the moon,' said Katharine softly.

'Nay, then you lie, it is the blessed sun,' Petruchio said.

'Then, God be blessed, it is the blessed sun,' cried Katharine. 'But sun it is not, when you say it is not, and the moon changes even as your mind. What you will have it named, even that it is, and so it shall be so for Katharine,' and then it was as though a sunburst lit them all, for Katharine smiled. And Katharine was smiling at Petruchio.

'Petruchio, the field is won,' whispered Hortensio, admiringly.

They held a feast in old Baptista's house to celebrate. There was, in the end, much to celebrate.

Lucentio, the real Lucentio, had seized the empty field and sprinted to the finishing post with scholar's robes and Latin texts alike abandoned. And when Baptista learned that the fortune promised to Bianca by Tranio was none other than his Latin master's own, all opposition dissolved in the predictable good humour of a satisfied father-in-law. And so Lucentio got to marry Bianca.

Hortensio had lost no time in courting his lusty widow, and was married to her already.

And Petruchio and Katharine seemed, even to those who did not know, to have achieved a kind of equilibrium, though how, following that extraordinary wedding, none was sure. Family and friends looked on with curiosity.

The feast was jovial, the talk was merry; and when the ladies finally withdrew and left the men to their own conversation, the talk was not surprisingly, of wives.

'Now, in good sadness, son Petruchio,' said Baptista, shaking his head, 'I think you have the veriest shrew of all.'

Petruchio, who knew better, would have none of this. In a trice a bet was laid, whose wife would come first if sent for: twenty crowns on it! No, more, said confident Petruchio. A hundred then! Done!

First Lucentio sent for Bianca. Bianca's answer: she was busy and she could not come. Next Hortensio. The widow's answer, back as quick: she suspected he was playing some joke and would not come.

Now Petruchio: the others waited eagerly to see the shrew's reply.

'What is your will, sir, that you send for me?' Katharine's soft tones enquired, and she stood before her husband with a smile upon her face. At once Petruchio sent her to fetch the other wives, who came with scowling faces and ill-tempered looks as matched the Katharine of old, and showed up ill before the serenity of the new Kate.

'Katharine,' said Petruchio, 'tell these headstrong women what duty they do owe their lords and husbands.'

'Come, come, you're mocking,' scorned Hortensio's wife. 'We will have no telling.'

'Come on, I say,' Petruchio repeated firmly to Katharine.

Katharine looked with curiosity towards her husband. What was it that Petruchio wanted? What was it that was being asked of her? And then she looked again towards Hortensio's bride, her face ugly with disgruntlement, her figure stiff with principled defiance of these men and most particularly of her new husband . . . and Katharine understood. She saw Petruchio's call to her as a call of loyalty and love: a statement to them all of how she knit with him and he with her.

The widow's face, grown purple with annoyance, looked much as she herself might once have done. 'Fie, fie!' Katharine cried. 'Unknit that threatening unkind brow, and dart not scornful glances from those eyes to wound your lord! It blots your beauty as frosts do bite the meadows; a woman moved is like a fountain troubled, muddy, ill-seeming, thick, bereft of beauty; and while it is so, none so dry or thirsty will deign to sip or touch one drop of it! Your husband is one that cares for you, and for your maintenance commits his body to painful labour both at sea and land, to watch the night in storms, the day in cold, and craves no other tribute at your hands but love, fair looks and true obedience: too little payment for so great a debt!'

With that she turned a look of such generous loyalty upon Petruchio, that even he was quite amazed, and cried out, 'Why, there's a wench! Come on, and kiss me, Kate!' Though he had looked to find a wife to make him rich with coins, now he saw that he was rich in more, much more, for Katharine had given him her heart, and that was wealth enough for any man.

'Come, Kate, we'll to bed,' he murmured, gently, and took her by the hand. And off they went together, the fortune-hunter and the shrew, transformed to tender husband, tender wife.

High up in the gallery of a lord's manor house, the tinker's dream had also reached its end.

Or had it?

The Tempest

It was like the frenzy of a raging animal, this dark fury of wind and sea that seized the ship. Thunder like the crack of doom; the flare of lightning across the decks; flames engulfed the cracking mast, tore down the sails into a blazing furnace that belched out panic-stricken passengers. Shouting, pounding feet, wrenching arms and smoking clothes: captain and sailors wrestled with their burning vessel and its shrieking cargo: a king, a prince, a duke, and lords . . .

But what did a royal cargo matter to that fury of wind and sea? Could a king's command throw back those mountainous waves? Could a lord's great wealth buy life or death before that tempest? In that storm there were no great and small, no rich or poor, no kings or sailors – only men, who shrieked before the thunder's power and knew their end had come.

The ship burned like a funeral pyre, split, was engulfed in a final, savage swell, and sank . . .

The watchers, high above it on a rocky headland, gazed upon the sight in silence. Nothing but scattered splinters on a foaming surface.

The one, a girl, stood pale with shock, in tears. Every angle of her huddled body spoke her misery at each pitiful cry of helpless men.

Her companion stood, unmoving. There was no trace of pity, joy or sorrow on his face. It was an old face, etched with the lines of time and scored with a lifetime's wisdom. And in his eyes . . . in his eyes there were glimmerings, flickerings, mysterious lights that echoed the silver of his hair and beard, gold, like the gold of a sunrise yet to come, red, like the fire that had consumed the ship, blue, like the sea lit by the lightning's flash . . .

In his eyes there was a story yet untold . . . it stirred angrily within him as he watched the dying ship.

He wore a robe, dark, rich and heavy. And though he stood

unmoving, the garment swayed, a strange, rhythmic movement of deep folds like secret caverns ripe with mysteries: fear, hope, knowledge, all were woven deep within its fabric, for there was magic in the web of it.

In his hand the old man held a staff, a gnarled wooden stick. Yet it was more . . . much more. It waited in his hand, as though it rested, as though no more than thought, no more than an eyelid's wink or the closing of an old man's hand, would fire its length with secret power . . .

And at his side there lay a book, red-bound and heavy, its pages old and worn with use, thumbed, scored, and learned, for they were pages saturated with the secrets of the enchanter's art.

The enchanter sighed, and turned towards the girl, whose pleading voice had broken through the dream which held him, silent, watching.

'If by your art, my dearest father, you have put the wild waters in this roar, calm them,' his daughter begged. She began to weep again, 'Poor souls, they perished. Had I been any god of power . . .'

Her father placed a calming hand against her cheek. 'Tell your piteous heart there's no harm done. No harm,' he repeated softly, and looked again towards the bay. The ship was gone. The winds were quieting . . .

It had begun. He drew his cloak about him, close, and held the staff, strong, firm, before his face . . . he closed his eyes, and from the earth, the sky, the winds, he felt the powers flowing anew.

It had begun.

He turned towards his daughter with sudden resolution.

'It is time.' He said it quietly, but with such force that instantly the girl grew quiet. 'I should inform you further,' he went on. 'Lend me your hand, and pluck my magic garments from me.'

Obediently the young girl grasped the heavy robe and eased it from her father's shoulders. She laid it gently to one side.

'Lie there, my art,' her father murmured. He took her gently by the shoulders, led her to a rock, and bid her sit on it. 'Wipe your eyes: have comfort.'

Wonderingly she did so. Trustingly she looked up at him, and waited. And so the enchanter began the tale: the tale that wrote its bitterness behind his eyes. This wreck that she had seen was conjured by his magic art. The storm was no more than a magician's fancy, conjured from the sky and sea by Prospero, the enchanter. She stared in wondering horror: could her beloved father be a man to kill for fancy?

But no, his gentle voice calmed her again, his gentle eyes reassured her, his gentle voice told on: not a single man was lost from that burned ship; every man still lived, as healthy as he had been the moment that the storm had caught them. And every man believed he had miraculously survived the sinking of a ship, while all the others drowned . . .

Yet, truly, not a single hair of any head was even wet. Prospero nodded with a kind of pride at her amazement. Now was the beginning . . .

It was also the end. Twelve years of preparation, twelve years of study, twelve years in which every bone and sinew, every thought, hope, desire had been sharpened to this moment . . . twelve years were drawing to a close. The hour had come when he must tell Miranda why.

It had begun a long time ago, in events long past, before ever they had come to dwell here on this island.

Did she remember such a time?

There were stirrings of faint memory, things far off but dream-like, the scattered remnants of a picture in a baby's mind: the half-remembered images of many women once attending her . . .

Prospero nodded: it had been so. 'Twelve years ago, Miranda, twelve years ago your father was the Duke of Milan and a prince of power.'

Miranda frowned in puzzlement. 'Sir, are you not my father?'

Prospero nodded. He gazed, with eyes of love, upon his innocent daughter. What would she make of the tale he had to tell; could her unresisting heart and loving spirit comprehend such evil? His face grew dark and bitter with the memory: trust betrayed and love turned sour; greed, ambition, murder . . .

Twelve years ago. A time when he, Prospero, was the noble Duke of Milan, the ruler of the most powerful of all the states. And this gentle girl, Miranda, no more than a child of three, a princess . . .

Duke Prospero of Milan had a brother, Antonio. In all the world Prospero had loved no one as he loved Miranda and Antonio. And he had trusted Antonio, as one could trust a beloved brother.

Prospero was a man of learning. He grew fascinated more and more each day by all his studies, drawn deep into his books, succumbing to his overwhelming thirst for knowledge. Each day his library absorbed him more than the affairs of state. He became removed from the daily duties of government, divesting his power instead on Antonio, to rule the land for him . . .

Antonio took the power, and wielded it for Prospero. He learned to revel in the control of men . . .

There came a time when it was not enough for him merely to act as duke and hold the keys of power in trust for Prospero. He yearned instead to *be* the duke, to wield that power, absolute power, for himself, and for himself alone.

'For me, poor man,' Prospero spoke quietly, and his face was greyed with memory, 'my library was dukedom large enough.'

And so the trusted brother Antonio, grown rotten with ambition, plotted with the King of Naples, a man long jealous of Milan's great wealth and power. One treacherous midnight, Antonio threw open the city gates and let the enemy in. For this treachery, the conquering King of Naples made Antonio Duke of Milan in Prospero's place.

Yet Antonio did not dare to kill his brother openly. By night he smuggled Prospero to the coast; with Miranda, then no more than three years old, he cast him out into the sea aboard a rotten carcass of a boat, barely afloat, without mast or sail, to let the pitiless sea do what Antonio dared not.

But they survived, through Prospero's strength and a little unexpected kindness: there was one man among the enemy, named Gonzalo, who had taken pity on their plight and given them a little food and water. He had also secretly provided clothes and other necessities, and knowing how Prospero loved his books, had smuggled into the boat some of his most prized volumes from his library.

Prospero stopped. His tale was drawing to its close.

'Here in this island we arrived . . .' He rose now, and lifted the magic robe about his shoulders.

He had returned to his beginning: the storm, the wreck.

Miranda waited. What reason could her father have for these?

Prospero smiled, and though to Miranda it was her father's gentle smile, yet there was nothing gentle in it. It was the smile that told again of twelve long years of preparation for this moment; twelve long years to perfect his enchanter's arts . . .

Now he was ready. Fortune smiled on him and brought his enemies to the shore of Prospero's island. That king on board that tormented ship was Alonso, King of Naples; that same king who had overthrown a rightful duke and placed his vicious brother on the throne. That prince was none other than the King of Naples' son. There was the king's brother, too, Sebastian.

Above all, there was Antonio, the man whole stole a brother's dukedom and threw him and his child into the waves to die . . .

Prospero raised a hand to stop Miranda's exclamation. 'Here cease more questions.' He placed his hand upon her head, with gentle touch. 'You are inclined to sleep; I know you cannot choose . . .'

Beneath the magician's spell, Miranda's eyes grew heavy, her eyelids dropped, and obediently she slept.

Now Prospero stood alone. One hand held his robe outstretched, the other held the staff high into the wind. He lifted his face towards the sky, and closed his eyes.

'Come away, servant, come. I am ready now. Approach, my Ariel, come,' he sent the call out from his mind.

There was a shimmer across the air, a silent whispering, a rustle as of a sea-breeze that kissed the sands and trilled its music in the leaf-fronds . . . and his servant came, a thing of glancing light, of movements quick as sight, of sounds like murmuring brooks . . .

'All hail, great master! Hail! I come to answer thy best pleasure: be it to fly, to swim, to dive into the fire, to ride on the curled clouds . . .'

Eagerly the master greeted him. Had the tempest been performed exactly as he asked; was every instruction followed?

Eagerly the servant-spirit answered: flying as flames, he had burned along the boat, brought lightning, thunderclaps, the mountainous waves, till all on board were mad with terror and all except the sailors plunged into the sea to escape the fires. First had been the king's son, Ferdinand, crying, 'Hell is empty, and all the devils are here!'

And yet – this was the master-stroke – they were all safe, all dry on land, miraculously not a hair damaged or out of place, their garments glossier and fresher than before. But they were scattered in groups across the island, each being certain that all others must be dead.

All had been done by Ariel, exactly as his master, Prospero asked.

The king's son, Ferdinand, had been brought ashore alone. He was now lodged in a deserted corner of the island, plunged in deep melancholy at his plight, mourning the loss of father, friends and ship alike.

The sailors were all safely stowed on board the ship (on which there was no trace of fire). Instead it nestled in a sheltered corner of the bay, hidden from the island by curtaining mists. Below her decks the sailors slept a deep, charmed sleep.

Prospero sighed. All faithfully done. 'But there's more work,' he spoke urgently. It was past midday, already two o'clock. 'The time between now and six must by us both be spent most preciously.'

Yet Ariel was restless. He had performed the tasks exactly as the enchanter ordered. Now the promised reward hung, tantalising, just beyond his reach: his liberty. Prospero had promised he could have his liberty when this day's work was done. Twelve years Ariel had served the enchanter faithfully, against that promise.

The reminder angered Prospero. Though he had lost all to the savagery of ambition and greed for power, yet now he, in his turn, wielded power mercilessly on those he needed for his arts. Until those arts had bent their powers towards the purpose for which he bred them, that power would stay absolute.

'Do you forget from what a torment I did free you?' he thundered. 'Have you forgotten the foul witch Sycorax?'

It was enough. Ariel trembled, remembering. The witch Sycorax was once ruler of this island, and Ariel her servant. For refusing to obey her foul commands, she had in a fit of anger shut him in a deep cleft in a pine-tree. There, in terrible agony, Ariel writhed for twelve long years. The witch had died, and on the island there was no one to hear his pitiful groans, except the witch's son, Caliban, a creature born of the witch's union with the devil, but without the witch's powers . . .

'It was my art that made the pine gape wide and let you out!' Prospero's call to loyalty and obedience hung, threatening, in the air.

And the air grew still, for Ariel was silent. Then, 'I thank thee, master,' came the whisper on the breeze.

'If you murmur more,' warned Prospero, 'I will split an oak and peg you in his knotty entrails till you have howled away twelve winters!'

'Pardon master, I will obey commands, and do my spiriting gently,' Ariel swore.

'Do so,' the sorcerer's voice grew gentle too. 'And after two days I will discharge you. Go now. Transform yourself into a nymph of the sea. Go take this shape, and return . . .'

The spirit flew, and Prospero bent to wake Miranda. There was still more to do, if all was to be accomplished as he planned within the hours before six . . .

'We'll visit Caliban my slave,' he told her. She shrank a little from this task, for there had been a time, long in the past, when Caliban, the witch's son, had sought to harm her. The fear lodged deep within her memories . . .

Caliban was Prospero's slave now, and he had need of him, just as the spirit Ariel was needed for this day's tasks. But Caliban's tasks were not the magic conjurings of Ariel; they were the services of daily need: to fetch their wood and make their fire . . .

Now Prospero hurried his reluctant daughter towards a hovel built below a jutting rock. It crouched there, low and dark and evil-smelling.

'What, ho! slave! Caliban! You earth, you! Speak!' his voice rang out.

There came a snarl, as of an animal, 'There's wood enough within.'

'Come forth, I say!' Prospero grew angry. 'There's other business for you! Come, you tortoise!'

A growl for answer, and the slow shufflings of a heavy body . . .

Ariel, like a sea-nymph, returned, took a whisper from the enchanter's mouth and was gone again about some new, important task, and only Prospero had seen him.

'You poisonous slave,' cried Prospero again into the hovel's dark interior and Miranda drew back a little, as she always did . . .

A bent, misshapen figure stumbled into view, his mouth drawn back on snarling teeth, his red-rimmed eyes fixed, burning, on his tormenter. Caliban hated Prospero with an all-consuming passion. Yet he feared him more, for any disobedience to the enchanter's will was swiftly punished with jabbing pains and cramps that tortured every bone and sinew of his twisted body.

On this island, it was never forgotten that Prospero had absolute power: Prospero was master, and ruthlessly he ruled these two, his servants, Caliban and Ariel.

Caliban stood before him, sullen, beaten, yet snarling still.

'This island's mine, by Sycorax my mother,' he hissed. 'When you came first, you stroked me and made much of me, would give me water with berries in it . . .' For that brief moment, the creature's eyes grew soft again and lost their hate, 'and then I loved you and showed you all the qualities of the isle, the fresh springs, the barren place and fertile.'

But now the hate returned, and savagery. He fixed a haunted eye on Prospero, 'cursed be I that did so! All the charms of Sycorax, toads, beetles, bats, light on you!' And the beaten creature that had once been lord of all the island, turned to lumber back into the prison rock in which the enchanter kept him. 'You taught me language,' he hissed, 'and my profit on it is, I know how to curse you! The red plague rid you for teaching me your language!'

But now he halted, trembling, for he could see that Prospero's anger flamed, and following Prospero's anger there was always pain to make him howl with the wolves . . .

109

He waited, sullenly, to take his orders from his master. Fuel to be fetched, and then other services . . .

There was the lilt of music, the whirr of Ariel upon the breeze, a song that floated in the air and caught the listener with invisible bonds and drew him on . . .

'Come unto these yellow sands . . .' the spirit sang.

And the listener followed, stumbling in his effort to keep pace, losing the sounds, then finding them again, drawn on, ever on, as Prospero had ordered, towards the enchanter's cave.

It was Ferdinand, the King of Naples's son. And a fine gentleman he was, tall, young and strong, richly dressed and handsome, though his eager face was somewhat shadowed with his sorrows. He had been sitting on a bank, mourning the wreck and his father's death when strange music had crept by upon the waters and snaked into his mind.

'Sure it waits upon some god of the island,' the young man breathed. . . . There the strains again. They floated about his head, now to this side, now the other . . .

'Full fathom five thy father lies;

Of his bones are coral made;

Those are pearls that were his eyes . . .' sang Ariel. The young man stopped in wonderment and awe. Surely this could be no earthly sound, no sound from human voice!

Miranda, seated as her father placed her, ready (though she did not know it) for this meeting, saw the young man enter the clearing before their cave, and with a gasp of shock and wonderment, leapt to her feet. In her young life she had only ever seen her father's white beard and wrinkled face and the twisted form of Caliban.

'What is it?' she cried to Prospero. 'A spirit? Lord, how it looks about! It is a spirit!'

'No,' Prospero smiled at her. 'It eats and sleeps and has such senses as we have. This gallant was in the wreck. He has lost his fellows and strays about to find them.'

Miranda stared. She drank in the sight. She feasted her eyes on the beauty of the figure. Surely a god!

Prospero saw that she was captured, and was pleased. All was as he desired, all as he planned, and he gave secret thanks to invisible Ariel hovering near, 'Spirit, fine spirit! I'll free you within two days for this!'

Ferdinand had seen Miranda. This prince was a much-travelled young man, accustomed to the rich beauties who graced the royal courts of Europe. Yet this vision of a windblown girl caught in a sunlit glade, fixed him in wonderment where he stood. It seemed to him as though he had never seen such beauty. It glowed like the sun itself. Surely this must be the goddess of this isle, she who conjured enchanted music from the air.

But then the goddess spoke, and told him she was nothing but a girl, and miraculously, he understood the words!

In relief and gratitude, Prince Ferdinand tumbled out the story of the wreck and all hands lost with it, his father's death, who he was, who else was on the ship . . . of Antonio, Duke of Milan . . .

At mention of his usurping brother's name, Prospero's eyes narrowed and pangs of anger filled him like the hot pains he cast on Caliban.

But there was much else to be done, before the end . . .

And first, his powers must be used on Ferdinand. This was his first and prime design, all for Miranda. He had seen the love already flowing between these two for every look that passed between them spoke of it. He had drawn Ferdinand here for this, and he was happy with it.

But love could be misplaced, and love could be betrayed, and Prospero's life was testimony to this . . . before Ferdinand could win Miranda as a wife, his love must stand the test of strength and constancy and truth and honesty. It must be fought for . . .

The two young people, entirely innocent of their parts in Prospero's grand design, were lost in pure admiration of each other's qualities. Prospero raised his voice. They did not hear. He brought the rasp of harshness into it. They heard. He accused the prince of lying, of coming as a spy to seize the island from them . . .

'No, as I am a man,' cried Ferdinand.

To Miranda, of course, the point was very simple. There was no evil that could dwell within a temple of such beauty as this man was. If an evil spirit had so fair a house, why then, good things would strive to dwell with it!

'Follow me,' said Prospero, brusquely. He wanted her to have such innocence and faith in human kind, he wanted her to have conviction in her love. But she must not be hurt, as he was . . . she must be strengthened, tested and tried.

'Come!' he ordered Ferdinand. 'I'll chain your neck and feet together: seawater you shall drink; your food shall be the fresh-brook muscles, withered roots and husks in which the acorn cradled. Follow!' he cried again, bringing to his face a look more terrible than he had shown before.

It did not frighten Ferdinand, who instantly drew his sword, and was as swiftly frozen as he stood, with sword raised high, by Prospero's magic.

And so they went on: Miranda pleaded with all her heart for Ferdinand; Prospero's face took on a frown of stern, unbending harshness; Ferdinand stared wonderingly at arms and legs grown heavy, refusing to move at his command, as he had always (not unreasonably) expected them to do. But he bore his trials bravely, declared that he could bear all hardship lightly if he could see the face of this sweet maid just once a day!

'It works,' breathed Prospero, the old enchanter who heard everything. And then to Ariel, he promised through his mind, 'You shall be as free as mountain winds: but then exactly do all points of my command.'

'To the syllable,' came Ariel's wind-blown music . . .

In a green, sunlit glade they gathered, a king, nobles, lords, all saved miraculously from watery death, all gorgeously attired in silks, brocades and velvets quite unstained by salt-sea wave . . .

There was understandably some debate about the nature of their situation. One old man, a wizened, bespectacled counsellor to the King of Naples, was hopeful. He was of the opinion that much thanks should be given and much merriment displayed. They were not dead: a miracle, no less!

Alonso, King of Naples, would not be convinced. He sat, plunged in misery. His son was dead. There was no shifting him from this conviction.

'Weigh our sorrow with our comfort,' the old counsellor urged Alonso.

'Peace!' Alonso begged the counsellor.

'He receives comfort like cold porridge,' observed Alonso's brother, Sebastian, nastily. To Sebastian there were no comforts to be found here, between wilting kings who muttered of lost sons, and elderly counsellors who chattered like ancient parrots. It mattered not to

Sebastian that the air was delicate and sweet, all growing things were green and lush . . .

King Alonso moaned again: a vision of his son had floated through his mind, wound grotesquely with seaweed from the ocean bed, dead! What strange fish might make his meal on him?

The old counsellor was, however, an ever optimistic man. He was in fact that same man named Gonzalo who had saved Prospero and Miranda from certain death twelve years before. But these events were lost far in the misting recesses of his memory. His old eyes gazed about him at the sunlit place, at rich, dark soil, at foliage lushly green; he drew the soft winds deep into his lungs, and his eyes grew dreamy, thinking of the world that might be built in such a paradise.

In such a world that he would build, all argument would disappear, and there would be no causes for it, no trade, no magistrates, no riches and no poverty, no boundaries, no work: all men would be equal, all; and women too, but innocent and pure; no sovereignty . . .

'Yet he would be king of it,' sneered Sebastian, to whom a world in which there were no riches to be seized would be a poor, boring world indeed.

The old man's dream grew brighter; he looked up and for his pains saw only mocking Sebastian and Antonio, who saluted him and called him king, while on the true king's face nothing showed but blank despair that emptied his shaking head of everything else.

But Prospero had heard enough: now he sent Ariel among them, to float unseen and fill the glade with mournful music, dark tones that filled their eyes with heaviness, dragged down their limbs, so that one by one they fell asleep.

But not all of them. There was another scene in Prospero's drama shortly to be acted: Sebastian and Antonio remained awake.

To a discerning eye, these two could not easily be told apart. Antonio was a brother turned a thief, betrayer of a brother's trust. Sebastian was brother to a king, shortly to betray a brother's trust, for he was a most ambitious man, with cold and calculating eyes.

And here they were, marooned on a deserted island (so they thought) beyond reach of any court or palace, far from the powers of Naples or Milan. Here, where as yet they had secured neither food nor drink, shelter nor any means of getting off the island (ignorant as they were of their ship, still hidden in the mists); where life might rest upon one man's help to another, these two remained true to their own natures: they could think only of a single method of advancement, even here in the sunshine of a tiny island basking in the sea. First Antonio (being a man ever alert to opportunity for self-advancement) and then Sebastian, quickly convinced by his faster-thinking fellow, cast their eyes on their companions fast asleep, and in particular on a weak-kneed king and dream-filled hopeful counsellor, and worked out that if both of these were killed (the king's son Ferdinand already being dead) . . . why then, Sebastian could be King of Naples, and Antonio rise to power with him . . .

Enough said: two swift murders, and the power would be theirs . . .

From afar the enchanter saw and heard their plot. Once again the games of power would be played with life and death as toys . . .

But this time the loser would be Gonzalo, once his friend! In no more than the winking of an eye, Ariel was despatched to wake Gonzalo and the king.

Caught with drawn swords and guilty faces, Sebastian and Antonio

muttered nervously of bellowing bulls (or was it roaring lions) against which they drew their weapons.

And from afar, Prospero's eyes glittered. It was all as he remembered, and all as he designed . . .

Caliban toiled along the beach beneath the load of wood, muttering. He cursed and spat with every grunting movement. Hatred for his master drove him, like a fire. His brain ached with memories of all the years of torment under Prospero. Years of spirits conjured, now like biting apes, now like hissing snakes, thousand upon thousand agonies from pricks and pinches, pains and cramps, in every bone and muscle of his body . . .

He stopped. A figure came towards him, a queer shape in jingling cap and tattered, flapping colours. It chattered, stumbled, mumbled, cowered, trembled, shook a bony fist towards the sky . . .

To Caliban, all figures were but spirits sent by Prospero to torture him for hauling in the wood too slowly. In a fit of terror he fell to the ground and flung his tattered cloak across his head, in the vain hope that it would make him invisible . . .

The figure was no spirit. It was another bewildered survivor from the wreck that never happened: Trinculo, aging court jester to the King of Naples, miraculously preserved, but facing as he believed, imminent eclipse from freshly brewing storms. Could one escape death twice?

There was more rumbling thunder, distant, growing closer, ominous.

Trinculo winced. 'If it should thunder as it did before, I know not where to hide my head: that same cloud cannot choose but fall by pailfuls,' he wailed, and clutched his arms about his thin shoulders, running from it.

Then he saw the bundle on the ground. He lurched to a halt. He pushed it cautiously with his toe. What was it? Man or fish? Dead or alive?

A fish: it smelt like a fish, undoubtedly. A very ancient and fish-like smell . . .

A sudden roll of thunder made the aging jester jump. The storm again! Weighing the stench of a fish-like dead or alive creature against the terrors of a blackening sky which burned a ship to cinders, he chose the fish, and with his bony nose pinched tight against the stench, he crept under the hairy cloak.

Caliban, frozen with horror at the nearness of a torturing spirit sent from Prospero, lay rigid, playing dead.

Towards this four-legged, four-armed hairy bundle on the beach, there came another apparition, one that swayed and tripped, hiccupped, paused, to undertake with utmost care the important task of swigging from a bottle, before progressing onwards, burping out a song . . .

'I shall no more to sea, to sea,
Here shall I die ashore . . .'

It was Stephano, the King of Naples' butler, who had floated to land on a wine barrel and had been filling his bloated stomach ever since. He stumbled across the large, hairy, smelly, solid looking something lying in this path. He staggered back. It did not move. By careful bending of his back he managed, though with difficulty, to bring his eyes to focus on it. And then, for no good reason, except that it was in his way, he gave it a hefty kick, reeled with this supreme effort, and fell with a gurgling squelch into the sand.

Whereupon Caliban, believing this to be some new and dreadful overture to torture from the spirits, let out a howl of misery.

The drunken butler heaved himself to his knees. He crawled towards the howl and pushed his bleared eyes close to the stinking bundle. A four-armed, four-legged howling creature! It moaned. Stephano concluded it must be some island monster in a fever. He hauled himself into a sitting position. The monster groaned in terrified anticipation.

An island monster, thought Stephano, cured and tamed, might yet be heaved back to Naples; and what a present for an emperor! He raised his bottle to the threatening clouds and drank to that, then prodded the monster for good measure.

'Do not torment me, I'll bring my wood home faster,' Caliban begged beneath the cloak.

'He's in a fit now,' announced Stephano. 'He shall taste of my bottle.' He nodded sagely at this thought, for the bottle was without question the cure for any ill. So saying he stuck the bottle in the monster's mouth, and leapt in sudden shock to find it was a monster of such delicate skill that it could suddenly, upon drinking, produce two voices, one in the top end (where a man could expect to hear a voice) and one in the bottom end that, when filled up with wine, miracles of miracles,

called him by his own name!

Being a brave man, he pulled at the monster's smaller legs (leaving the large, hairy ones alone) and discovered, to his pleasure, no less than his good friend Trinculo. Whereupon the two friends danced and swayed for joy and compared notes on their escape from a watery grave.

Caliban had meanwhile begun to experience a warm inner glow that seemed uncannily connected to that bottle. He gazed upon it wonderingly and upon the portly man in tattered breeches who nursed the magic potion lovingly.

'Have you not dropped from heaven?' he asked.

'Out of the moon, I do assure you,' chortled Stephano.

It was enough for Caliban: this was a god, dropped from the heavens with potions that could lift a man from earth and make him fly . . .

He fell to his knees before his god, 'I'll show you every fertile inch of the island: I will kiss your foot . . .' he pledged, and did so. 'I'll show you the best springs, I'll pluck you berries, I'll fish for you and get you wood enough . . .' And in his overflowing love he offered this god all, all his worldly wealth, all the riches of this kingdom that should be his, as once he had to Prospero!

And then, remembering, he yelled with sudden fury, 'a plague upon the tyrant that I serve! I'll bear no more sticks for him, but follow you, you wondrous man!'

'A most ridiculous monster, to make a wonder of a poor drunkard,' observed Trinculo the jester, blinking.

'Lead the way,' cried Stephano, game for anything. 'Trinculo, the king and all our company being drowned, we will inherit here. This will be our kingdom! Bear my bottle,' he said to Caliban, majestically, and Caliban took the bottle as though it were a delicate jewel nestling on a gilded cushion, and held it up aloft, and led them, singing . . .

'Farewell, master; farewell, farewell!
Ban, Ban Cacaliban,
Has a new master: get a new man . . .
Freedom, hey-day! hey-day, freedom! freedom, hey-day, freedom!'

Ferdinand was still Prospero's prisoner, still toiling at fetching and carrying logs, thousand upon thousand upon thousand. Prospero had set him Caliban's work, to test Miranda in her love. Did handsome youths in gorgeous clothes, transformed to filth and sweat and rags, still shine for her? Or did Ferdinand at filthy work become a Caliban in her young eyes?

He did not. She wept to see him toil: she offered to do it for him; she begged him to rest whenever she thought her father was in his study; she found every excuse to visit him, and share his misery.

Ferdinand, being a king's son and unfitted for work of any kind, struggled beneath an unequal burden. But he was valiant: driven ever onward by sweet Miranda's loving sighs and wistful adoration, he manfully endured the trial.

And Prospero nodded with satisfaction. Their love was not turned astray by so much harshness; if anything, it grew bolder . . . Ferdinand swore he loved, prized and honoured Miranda above all else in the world. Miranda wept to hear it. 'I am your wife, if you will marry me,' she cried.

And Prospero almost wept in joy to hear Ferdinand's answering vow of love: they would be man and wife. Before the day was out, Miranda would be Queen of Naples. Soon, their trial would be done. Soon this act of the drama could be closed.

Stephano was playing king, and passed the bottle. Caliban drank, adored his god, and passed the bottle. Trinculo drank, jeered at Caliban, and passed the bottle.

Caliban told them of his master who had by sorcery seized the island. 'From me he got it,' Caliban cried, and hiccupped and stared through desperate eyes at god Stephano, 'If you will revenge it on him, for I know you dare,' he cried, 'you shall be lord of it and I'll serve you!'

Planted thus in Stephano's brain, the idea was good. Decorated here and there, with something of the customs of this master, and something of his possessions that would be worth having, and something about his books (without which he was powerless) and something of his pretty daughter, the idea was even better.

'Monster, I will kill this man: his daughter and I will be king and queen, and Trinculo and yourself shall be viceroys. Do you like the plot, Trinculo?'

'Excellent,' burped Trinculo.

And with the bargain laid, they shook hands on it, and passed the bottle, and Stephano sang the song again that he had just been teaching Caliban.

'Flout 'em and scout 'em,

And scout 'em, and flout 'em;

Thought is free.'

But to their consternation, the tune was changing, and without them doing anything! Strange, wistful sounds and lilting pipes drowned out their merry verse, and though they struggled manfully to hold a course, the ghostly music overwhelmed them . . .

'Oh forgive me my sins,' cried Trinculo, and tried to block his ears.

'I defy you,' yelled Stephano to the phantom musician, and then, more wisely, and just in case . . . 'Mercy upon us!'

'Are you afraid?' asked Caliban curiously. 'Be not afraid. The isle is full of noises, sounds and sweet airs, that give delight and hurt not.' A strange gentleness had come upon the creature as he spoke, a dreaming peace; it was as though, let loose, he melted once again into this island that was his. 'Sometimes a thousand twangling instruments will hum about my ears, and sometimes voices that, if I then had waked after long sleep, will make me sleep again; and then, in dreaming, the clouds would seem to open and show riches ready to drop upon me, that, when I waked, I cried to dream again!'

'This will prove a brave kingdom to me, where I shall have my music for nothing,' Stephano yelled, and gathered more courage from the bottle.

'When Prospero is destroyed,' Caliban reminded him. Caliban's island dream had gone, and the urgency of his escape from Prospero was all.

'The sound is going away,' cried Trinculo, bolder for the reminder of their paradise to come. 'Let's follow it and after do our work!'

'Lead, monster,' Stephano waved Caliban on, 'we'll follow . . .'

But Ariel, musician of the air, had heard their plot, and swift as a salt-sea breeze across the bay had carried the news to Prospero: Caliban the slave had found a god, a god with a faded, jingling henchman by his side, and on the wings of ambition these three lurched towards him, bent on murder for the kingdom of the island.

Again the game of power was played, with life and death as toys.

With aching limbs, and sinking heart, the King of Naples sank to rest. There was no finding Ferdinand alive. Even the sea seemed to mock their search.

Around him all the lords and nobles faltered, too, as he did (for they were always quick to take their cue from him). Even old Gonzalo was beyond all cheerful words, for his old bones ached too much with tramping in a fruitless search.

Sebastian and Antonio, though, hovered close. They had forgotten nothing of their purpose. As soon as opportunity was there . . . Sebastian nodded to Antonio. Tonight . . . Antonio urged Sebastian.

Their secret dialogue broke off: they had heard strange, solemn sounds, like deep murmurs rising from the earth . . . They all moved nervously together and stared about. The air was growing misty. They huddled closer. From the gleaming centre of the mists came twisting shapes of beings, half animal, half human, grotesque to look at, yet they smiled, nodded, seemed courteous, and bore a banquet into the centre of the glade, table upon table piled with food, and then with nods and bows they melted back into air and only the echo of the music hung behind.

But they had left the feast behind! King and lords stared round the glade nervously. King and lords awaited further happenings. The glade was quiet. The lords were hungry, growing hungrier by the minute. Sebastian was all for eating. Alonso drew back nervously. Gonzalo, reassured by the politeness of the mysterious creatures, was for investigating further.

They moved towards the laden tables, cautiously . . .

A clap of thunder and the sear of lightning shot across the glade! A great bird swooped . . . a monstrous giant with a hag-like human face and the body of a taloned vulture, whose vast wings smote the table like a hammer blow, and instantly the banquet vanished.

'You are three men of sin,' the apparition cried, and the thundering voice was agony in their ears, 'on this island where man doth not inhabit, you amongst men being most unfit to live, *I* have made you mad!'

Fearing imminent death, Sebastian and Antonio drew swords . . . 'You fools!' the terrible voice rang out again. 'I and my fellows are ministers of Fate: your swords may as well wound the loud winds, or kill the waters, as diminish one feather in my plume!' And the voice rose to the rumbling of an earthquake, the trees and rocks about them seemed to shake before its wrath. 'But remember . . .' the warning hung ominously in the air. 'Remember . . . You three did supplant good Prospero from Milan: for which foul deed, the powers have incensed the seas and shores, yes, all the creatures, against your peace. They have bereft thee, Alonso of thy son, and by me they do pronounce a lingering torture, worse than any death, shall step by step attend you and your ways.'

There was a roll of thunder so deafening and the light so blinding, that they hid their heads, and when they looked again, the bird had gone.

In his wake soft music played to mock them, the shimmering spirits of the air returned, and before their helpless eyes and helpless hands, taunting, the spirits danced, and carried out the table.

The glade was empty now, filled only with their terror.

Invisible above, Prospero, watched. Now let the terror work. Now let their agony of fear bore madness deep within each villainous heart . . .

The time had come for Prospero to release Ferdinand. But being so close now to the end, the enchanter wished to give one final gift to these young people, to reveal the wonders of his powers, before the end, to them.

He closed his eyes, and through his mind he sent the call: 'Spirits, which by my art I now call up,' he cried, and rejoiced as his many spirits thronged about the united couple, now deep in love, dancing in celebration of the lovers: spirits of all the island's secret places, of the woods and trees, the streams and lapping seas, of hill and valley, sky and earth . . .

Then he froze. A thought, ice cold, had shot into his brain. In the warmth of the young people's love he had forgotten Caliban. He had forgotten the conspiracy against his life.

And with that memory, the warm visions of love and plenty he had conjured up, were gone. Ferdinand and Miranda stared in some dismay at Prospero, grown dark with bitterness again.

Prospero swiftly moved to reassure them.

'Be cheerful, sir. Our revels now are ended. These, our actors, were all spirits and are melted into air! We are such stuff as dreams are made on, and our little life is rounded with a sleep . . .'

But Caliban was coming, and he must prepare. Summoning Ariel, he gave commands . . .

He waited. Light as the sea-blown breeze, the spirit servant had returned, and in his arms there gleamed rich garments, all the colours of the rainbow. Prospero had charmed a storm, a wreck, a spirit-feast, to confuse and madden a treacherous king and villainous lords; he had brought forth a spirits' dance of blessing for young lovers, and now for drunken murderers, the vanity of gaudy clothes to deck a would-be king.

They were not so jovial as before, Stephano, Caliban and Trinculo. The ghostly music had led them a merry dance. They were pricked by thorns and briars, scratched, torn, smeared with mud, and now stinking, wet, and worst of all, had lost their bottle somewhere beneath the rancid scum of some filthy gurgling pond. Trinculo whined, and

Stephano bellowed, and Caliban grew more terrified by the minute that Prospero would hear them . . .

He might have saved his breath: Trinculo had seen the clothes. There was no stopping him. With a cry of ecstasy he fell upon them. Garments for a king, finery for a king's minister, riches beyond a jester's dreams!

'Let it alone, you fool,' hissed Caliban. 'It is trash.'

But already there was a battle royal between a would-be king and would-be minister: cavorting, squabbling, flourishing, snatching, . . . heads, arms, legs, thrusting in and out of sleeves and tearing necklines.

'Let's alone and do the murder first,' begged Caliban, 'if he awakes, from toe to crown he'll fill our skins with pinches!'

'Be you quiet monster,' ordered Stephano struggling for possession of a jacket.

'I will have none of it,' yelled Caliban, 'we shall lose our time, and all be turned to barnacles or apes!'

But it was neither apes nor barnacles for them. With blood-curdling baying of hunger, the snapping jaws of ravenous hunting dogs erupted from the forest, and before the snarling terror of those phantom beasts, the would-be killers fled . . .

Prospero and Ariel watched their quarry run. 'At this hour lie at my mercy all mine enemies,' triumphant Prospero spoke.

The final act was drawing near. 'Shortly shall all my labours end. And you, Ariel, shall have the air at freedom: for a little, follow, and do me service . . .'

The spirit bowed his head; the final act, and after, liberty . . .

'Now does my project gather to a head: my charms crack not – my spirits obey.' Prospero stood ready. Round his shoulders swayed his magic robe. And by his side stood Ariel. 'How's the day?' Prospero murmured to his faithful spirit servant.

'On the sixth hour; at which time, you said our work should cease.'

'I did say so, when first I raised the tempest.'

Since then: a king and treacherous brothers had been maddened with their guilt and fear, imprisoned at his will, locked fast by his charms.

The final power. His, they were, for life or death. The final choice now lay before him.

'Your charm so strongly works on them, that if you now beheld them, your affections would become tender,' Ariel's music reached into his mind. He stood quietly. 'Do you think so, spirit?' he asked.

'Mine would, sir, were I human,' the spirit said.

Silence grew about the enchanter and his tender servant spirit. The final choice must now be made.

But he was listening to Ariel's music. Finally he spoke. 'Go release them, Ariel,' the enchanter said. 'My charms I'll break, their senses I'll restore, and they shall be themselves.'

Joyfully, Ariel sped away. And Prospero stood alone. He closed his eyes, and spread his arms out wide so that the magic robe swirled, rich with power.

'I have bedimmed the noontide sun, called forth the mutinous winds, and between the green sea and the blue vault of the sky I have set roaring war: to the dread rattling thunder have I given fire . . . and by the roots plucked up the pine and cedar . . . graves, at my command have waked their sleepers, opened and let them forth . . .'

But here it would end. He knew that now. Here, when the final act was over.

He drew a magic circle, and into it they came, the maddened king, the staring brothers, the bewildered lords. They stood imprisoned in Prospero's enchantment, silent, asleep, awaiting the final vengeance.

Now they must see him as he was, when all began: as Prospero, one-time Duke of Milan.

Swiftly, Ariel fetched the clothes of Prospero the Duke, and singing, for his liberty was nearing and he almost danced with joy, he helped the old man to remove the robes of Prospero the enchanter. Now he stood as Prospero, the Duke.

Slowly, with no violence, Prospero released them from their sleep. They stared in disbelief: Prospero, long believed dead, now come back from the grave! And their minds, but a few minutes ago twisting in crazed terror, calm, and clear again!

There followed a scene of such bewilderment and awe, such recognitions, explanations, grief, remorse, apologies and reconciliation, as the island had never seen before, nor would it ever again. Alonso, King of Naples, who had long felt an inward torture for the deeds committed twelve long years ago, wept for sorrow at his villainy and begged forgiveness. Gonzalo was in ecstasies of joy, relief and amazement all in one.

Antonio and Sebastian, who in a trice had understood that Prospero

knew all and could, with but a single word, betray their villainy to
Alonso, now faced the ultimate of judges: their own consciences,
newly-sharpened by the terrors of this island magic.

But from them all, Prospero had one demand: the restoration of his
dukedom, lands, wealth and all rights.

Alonso, of course, still mourned the loss of Ferdinand: Prospero
drew back the curtains of his cave and revealed Miranda, ignorant of all
the excitement taking place outdoors. Quietly, and needing nothing
more, she played at chess with none other than the king's son Ferdinand.

More wonderment, embracing, joy, and explanations . . .

Miranda stared in rapture at the glorious array of gilded lords.

'How beauteous mankind is!' she cried. 'Oh brave new world, that
has such people in it!'

'It is new to you,' said Prospero, with a lifetime's weary knowledge.

They all still mourned the loss of sailors, captain, ship. One by one

125

they were produced, lifted through the balmy air and placed before them by invisible Ariel.

'Was it well done?' whispered Ariel to Prospero.

'Bravely,' whispered Prospero to Ariel. 'You shall be free. Set Caliban and his companions free; untie the spell.'

And so to the final revelation: the hapless trio stumbled in, limply hung with stolen clothes, and cowed and sheepish with it. Caliban, expecting vicious punishment, found in Prospero a new master, decked in unknown finery, and generous in forgiveness. Instantly he transferred his adoration to this better master, and wondered how he had ever adored a drunkard as a god.

So now, instead of vengeance, it was hospitality that Prospero offered. And on the morrow they would all embark for Naples to see the wedding of Ferdinand and Miranda; then would the final bond of reconciliation be tied. Then Prospero would turn for home, for Milan.

'I promise you calm seas, auspicious gales . . .' the enchanter murmured. And in his mind he called for the last time to Ariel. 'My Ariel, chick, that is your charge: then to the elements be free . . .'

There was a flutter in the breeze, as of a dragonfly's wings, and with a whisper of farewell and love to Prospero, the spirit flew to liberty . . .

Prospero stood alone, high on the rocky headland, in the dark. Ariel and Caliban were free: one to the winds, and one to his island paradise.

He had planned his magic all for vengeance: yet in the final hour it had brought him face to face with tenderness and charity. In the magic circle drawn for vengeance, he had seen his victims' misery was no less terrible than his own twelve years before, and he had seen his ruthless use of power no better than that abuse he suffered at their hands. That was the final music Ariel had played for him.

So now the sea would take his magic and bury it deep. First his robe, his book, and then his staff, broken in two, he cast into the waves.

For that brief, sharp moment, as he saw them fly from his hands, there was an unutterable despair. He was a man again, no more than a man. Gone was the magic which had given him power over earth, air, fire, water, life and death, and over an infinity of dreams . . .

But after the despair, there was a new peace: as a man he had the power of choice, of knowledge, understanding, compassion, pity, love. And in that there was untold richness, glory, hope . . . and dreams.